Scarcity by Design

2

Scarcity by Design

The Legacy of New York City's Housing Policies

Peter D. Salins and
Gerard C. S. Mildner

Harvard University Press
Cambridge, Massachusetts
London, England
1992

Library of Congress Cataloging-in-Publication Data
Salins, Peter D.
Scarcity by design : the legacy of New York City's housing
policies / Peter D. Salins and Gerard C. S. Mildner.
p. cm.
Includes bibliographical references and index.
ISBN 0-674-79018-9 (alk. paper)
1. Housing policy—New York (N.Y.) 2. Housing policy—New York
(State) I. Mildner, Gerard C. S. II. Title.
HD7304.N5S29 1992
363.5'8'097471—dc20
92-15981
CIP

to our wives, Rochelle and Lucia

Preface

This is a book about a common failing of government policy: devising a cure that is worse than the disease. The policy in this case concerns housing, and the government implementing it is that of America's largest, most sophisticated, and most intrusive municipality: New York City. The original disease still afflicts the city after half a century: it is that New York housing prices are higher than most New Yorkers think they should pay. And the cure has consisted of government regulations and subsidies designed to making housing cheaper. The result issuing from decades of this therapy—a therapy which in its scope is unique among American cities—has been the long, slow demise of New York's housing stock, leaving in its wake physical deterioration, nasty adversarial politics, and pervasive housing scarcity. Most disappointing, the therapy has not succeeded in its most worthy objective: making housing cheaper and better for the poor. To the extent that it has yielded any bargain-rate, decent apartments at all, they have been occupied primarily by those who could well afford to pay more.

Scarcity by Design, then, is the story of how five decades of New York City's policy nostrums have worsened, and in some cases instigated, most of the city's housing problems. Especially destructive has been the way various housing and related policies have interacted and negatively reinforced each other to distort the market and ruin the housing stock. But the book also suggests how, even at this late date, much of the damage might be repaired.

Even as a case study of a particular complex of unfortunate policies in a particular city, the book illustrates some larger and more universal lessons: with respect to housing policies in other cities, government intervention in other markets, and government over-reaching whenever it attempts to reorder behavior and events in domains it cannot easily control. That these lessons need to be learned is evident to us when we hear of policy proposals being suggested in cities and states around the nation. They echo New Yorkers' indifference to the imperatives of private markets, New Yorkers' eternal desire to get more than they pay for, and New Yorkers' faith that, with enough regulation and expenditure, government can and should solve most urban problems.

Acknowledgments

Like any co-authored book, this one has been a highly collaborative effort, requiring us authors to merge and complement each other's factual, conceptual, and theoretical perspectives. Thus it is only fitting for us to thank each other for maintaining the patience, cooperation, and friendship that saw the project through. We also want to thank Mark Riebling and Richard Vigilante, who helped us to reconcile our somewhat disparate writing styles and ensure an overall consistency and logical flow in the narrative.

We would also like to thank those who provided research assistance, especially Joe Nelson, John Simkiss, Piero Tozzi, and Scott Wood. Thanks are due to Jack Richman, whose guidance and assistance were much appreciated.

We are most grateful to Michael Aronson, general editor of Harvard University Press, for his encouragement and faith in our manuscript. We also want to thank Anita Safran and other members of the staff.

Above all we wish to express our appreciation and gratitude to the Manhattan Institute, its president Bill Hammett, and vice-president Larry Mone, for offering the financial and logistical support without which the book could not have been written.

Peter D. Salins
Gerard Mildner

Contents

Scarcity by Design

The Vicious Cycle

All is not well with rental housing in New York City. On that point most New Yorkers will agree. In desirable neighborhoods of the city it is hard to find a nice apartment at a reasonable price. In the city's worst areas, where apartments may be somewhat cheaper, decent apartments are still scarce and far beyond the means of the families willing to live there. And the millions of New Yorkers who are already housed find their buildings poorly maintained and their surroundings crumbling with physical neglect and social pathology. Although the prevailing weakness of the city's real estate market since 1988 has eased rents and housing prices somewhat and allowed the vacancy rate to rise slightly, New York's housing condition is still characterized by low quality, pervasive scarcity, and excessive rents for available units.

These facts are confirmed in official statistics that document a historically low rate of housing construction dating back to well before the real estate slump, unacceptably high rates of housing loss which lead to public takeover of apartment houses for tax delinquency, and low vacancy rates. The dismal state of rental housing in New York threatens not only that intangible factor called the "quality of life;" it may well impair the vitality of the city's bread and butter—its economy—as businesses find it harder to recruit new employees or keep the ones they have.

The nearly universal complaints about New York's housing are generally accompanied by a nearly exhaustive list of human or institutional scapegoats. The city's poor housing conditions have been caused by the withdrawal of federal housing subsidies during the Reagan years. Or they result from the city's invasion by young professionals during the Wall Street boom, as they displaced poor families in gentrifying neighborhoods and bid up rents and housing prices everywhere. Or they are caused by rapacious landlords who exploit their tenants, willfully neglect their properties, and would rather co-op or warehouse their apartments than make them available at modest but still profitable rents. Or they are a byproduct of the unforgiving economics of housing which makes it impossible for private developers or landlords to provide affordable unsubsidized dwellings. The search for scapegoats, however, is misplaced. In the final analysis New York's housing woes are the product of New York's housing policies.

As it happens, New York City, with the active cooperation of New York State, has managed to build over a period of forty years, component by component, an elaborate policy machine that effectively, if inadvertently, is perfectly designed to weaken its private housing market. To be sure, each component of this machine was introduced with the best of intentions, and in every instance ostensibly to improve rather than worsen New York's housing conditions. But the good intentions have rested on a quicksand of wishful thinking, political expediency, constituent pressure, willful disregard of previous experience, and ignorance of the economics of housing. Reviewing the piecemeal implementation of the housing policy machine over the years, we follow a trail of interventions in the city's housing market and find that each new intervention has created additional problems requiring further measures to correct.

Each component in the overall machine of housing debilitation is predicated on its own internal logic. Each component weakens housing by itself, but operating in concert the components devastate the ability of New York's housing market to offer the quantity, quality, or price of housing necessary to provide decent shelter for all its households. These components, while comprised of many policies and programs, essentially fall under four major headings: rent regulation and its many spin-offs, land use regulation and its associated procedural and environmental embellishments, the public ownership and management of housing, and the system of property taxation and abatements.

Rent regulation began simply, if restrictively, four decades ago by freezing rents in New York's older housing stock at the beginning of a fairly long period of price stability. As the era of price stability came to a close, a flurry of measures was implemented that extended the harm of rent regulation from merely causing disinvestment in housing maintenance to discouraging any new mid-priced rental housing from being built and bringing a massive misallocation of the existing stock. Rent regulation's reach was extended in 1969 by the inclusion of virtually all dwellings not occupied by owners, and its depth was extended by adding layers of ever more restrictive procedural rules. Inflation has further widened the gap between regulated and market rents.

All attempts to temper rent regulation's impact on the profitability of rental housing have either been beaten back or vitiated in their implementation. The Maximum Base Rent (MBR) system, which was introduced in 1970 to close the regulation/market gap over an extended period, has been difficult to implement, contains vast loopholes of ineligibility, and often depends on flawed and obsolete assessments of market rents. The Major Capital Improvements (MCI) program launched in 1969 doesn't deliver rent increases commensurate with the cost of improvements. And the so-called vacancy decontrol program legislated in 1971, as modified in 1974, only transfers apartments from one form of regulation to another, often more stringent, system.

Land use regulation in New York, likewise, has been transformed from a relatively simple system designed to protect the public from a limited number of easily identifiable harms into a complex body of law that makes it exceedingly difficult for all but the biggest and hardiest developers to build anything, anywhere. While land use regulation is not targeted exclusively on housing, its impact on housing is greater than on any other development category because commercial and office construction more easily escapes some of the other constraints on profitability, most notably rent regulation.

The original 1916 zoning ordinance was enacted to restrain excessive density in Manhattan, to guarantee that light and air reached the streets and sidewalks, and to assure that radically incompatible land uses were not placed next to each other. In 1961 the ordinance was completely overhauled to reduce the total amount of developable space permitted, to reduce density at most locations, and to make property line setback and height limitations more stringent.

Most perversely of all, the 1961 zoning ordinance set out to reserve vast amounts of prime land for manufacturing activities just at the time that the need for manufacturing space was drastically declining.

But a more constraining zoning ordinance is only the tip of the iceberg. Several other land use regulatory rubrics have been super-imposed upon the zoning ordinance to narrow development possi-bilities to the vanishing point. A state-wide environmental review procedure—the State Environmental Quality Review Act (SEQRA) and the city's counterpart (CEQRA)—mandates an environmental impact statement (EIS) to justify, essentially, any large-scale project. By itself, completing an EIS is an expensive and time-consuming un-dertaking. But it can also pose more serious obstacles than the time and cost of its preparation. If the EIS discloses any adverse environ-mental impacts—traffic, noise, water or air quality degradation, or even the displacement of existing residents or businesses—the de-veloper must be prepared to mitigate these harms. Even if the EIS discloses no adverse impacts, such opponents of the development as community advocacy groups or owners of competing activities can challenge the accuracy of the EIS during the city's review process or in court, thus delaying or possibly killing the project.

Other more cumbersome land use laws have been implemented. The landmarks preservation law of the city can forestall new devel-opment in two ways. Old structures in a development site that would normally be cleared to make way for new construction may be designated as "landmarks" and thus prevent or distort a project. More intrusively, entire sections of the city such as Greenwich Vil-lage, Park Slope, and the Upper East Side have been designated as "landmark districts" where nothing can be built or altered with-out being subjected to elaborate, and often fatal, review by the Land-marks Commission. Any development project that manages to get by these various gauntlets and hurdles must still contend with the Uniform Land Use Review Procedure (ULURP), which creates fo-rums and opportunities for antagonistic local interest groups and politicians to challenge it.

What these various development impediments add up to, and what most distinguishes the New York City development climate from that of other American cities, is the virtual absence of what is called "as of right" building options. In other words, the restrictive-ness and overlapping of New York's land use laws make requests for exceptional treatment, and the concommitant subjective review process, the normal rather than the unusual case.

The third component impairing New York's housing market is the role of various public agencies as owners, managers, and developers of housing in their own right. The oldest and arguably the most benign of these agencies is the New York City Housing Authority, which owns and operates 165,000 apartments in public housing "projects." The NYCHA, largely at federal government expense, is supposed to provide decent housing for the poorest New York households, giving them an alternative to substandard slum dwellings. However, since the poorest New Yorkers also make the least satisfactory tenants in terms of project upkeep and social tranquility, the NYCHA attempts (against both the letter and the spirit of federal rules) to recruit as tenants the most affluent or best behaved of the "poor" for its projects. To the extent it succeeds in this effort, NYCHA robs the moderate-priced private housing market of many of its more economically viable potential tenants.

The state and city have also subsidized many housing developments explicitly targeted to moderate income families, which have had an even greater distorting impact on the private housing market. These have been built by a number of agencies under a variety of funding rubrics, the most extensive being the city and state Mitchell-Lama programs. By offering new, low rent and high quality apartments in middle income neighborhoods, such projects compete directly with the private market in exactly the price niche that unsubsidized development could reach. Why is this bad? Aside from wasting public revenues to build what the private sector could offer without subsidies, these developments withdraw a large segment of the city's housing market from the dynamics of filtering: the process by which housing built for middle income households at some point becomes available for lower middle income and poor families.

The most problematic public role, however, is New York City's ownership and management of more than 48,000 units of tax foreclosed housing. For over a decade the city government has had the distinction of being New York's premier slumlord. Since 1988 the city has embarked on an ambitious and incredibly costly program of paying for the rehabilitation of virtually its entire inventory. While renovated tenements are preferable to publicly owned slums, the city's 5.1 billion dollar housing program poses a number of serious problems for New York's housing market, both now and in the future. While most of the buidings to be "rehabbed" will nominally be under one form or another of private ownership, most of this stock will not really be part of the private housing market. Roughly half of these apartments will be operated by non-profit organizations, and the buildings in the other for-profit half will have their finances dependent on continuing deep subsidies and their operations constrained by a web of regulations. As such, this subsidized and regulated municipal housing sub-market will undercut the viability of the remaining privately owned low income rental stock, as well as feed an unsustainable and destabilizing appetite for public support of most low cost housing.

The fourth component of New York's moribund housing market is the city's property tax system. In the aggregate, New York's real property taxes are not excessive for a city of its size. However, the distribution of this tax burden significantly discourages the maintenance of the existing rental stock and the construction of new rental housing. The property tax system is tilted to minimize the taxes on owner-occupied one- to three-family homes in the better neighborhoods of New York's outer boroughs. The effect of this policy is to greatly increase the tax burden on all rental housing, but especially on rental housing in Manhattan and in the city's poorer areas. Making rental property absorb a disproportionate share of the property tax is especially harmful at the low end of the housing market. To the extent that owners can shift the incidence of the tax to their tenants, higher rents make apartments less affordable. For the most part, however, owners must absorb property taxes, a burden that leads them to neglect their properties or, if the tax burdens appear insupportable enough, to abandon them. Because an additional bias of New York's property tax system tilts against new structures of all kinds, the development of new rental housing is discouraged unless it is eligible for tax abatement. But tax abatements are not much of an answer because they require great diligence to secure, they come with onerous strings attached, and they gradually expire in any case.

The various elements of New York's troubled housing policy are generally viewed, favorably or critically, in isolation. They are, after all, administered by different sets of bureaucracies that rarely, if ever, communicate with one another. They are responsive to different vested interests and constituents. They evolve under the pressure of different exigencies and on different timetables. Nevertheless, they must be considered collectively because these policy elements feed into each other, and they powerfully reinforce each other's adverse impacts on the housing market. The scarcity of vacant apartments fostered by rent regulation makes subsidized middle income housing a political imperative. The stock of new subsidized apartments along-side the older regulated ones vitiates the demand for new privately built (and unsubsidized) mid-priced rental housing. But the economics of unassisted housing is also dealt a fatal blow on the supply side because of land costs elevated by restrictive development regulation, and property taxes raised by the inequitable pattern of assessment. The resulting dearth of new privately built housing provides the rationale for maintaining rent regulation and housing subsidies. And so it goes in a self-perpetuating and self-justifying cycle of housing market debilitation.

In addition, behind the idiosyncratic histories of the various housing policy components lurks a set of common assumptions rooted in the peculiar political culture of New York City and New York State. The most pervasive of these underlying commonalities is the skepticism of New York's politicians and their constituents regarding the applicability to housing of the more familiar axioms of economics. Surprisingly, even as the leaders of the most hidebound Communist autocracies of Eastern Europe have come to worship at the altar of free markets, and to accept microeconomic theory's admonitions regarding the harms arising from government regulation and price-setting, New York's political leaders still need to be convinced. Rent regulation is only the most blatant instance of a policy predicated on the belief that one can cheat the market and get away with it. But New York's policies in land use regulation, publicly owned housing, and property taxation also rest on a heedlessness of well-understood microeconomic incentives and disincentives.

New Yorkers' disregard of economic theory, in turn, is grounded in their fervent desire to get more than they pay for. New York's regulated tenants want quality housing at bargain prices. New York's planners want a wide variety of public and aesthetic amenities to be provided costlessly as a byproduct of development rather than at public expense. New York's housing administrators and advocates hope to sustain a large inventory of low cost housing, inhabited by families with middle class values, funded by owners of unsubsidized apartments or taxpayers outside of New York. And the biases of the property tax are generated by the barely disguised or excused efforts of middle and upper income homeowners outside Manhattan to shift their tax burden onto apartment dwellers, the business community, and Manhattan property owners.

However, vested interests and ordinary people in all cities might well prefer a free lunch to a costly one. And economic theory might not, by itself, persuade Americans anywhere to give up their perquisites. For these inclinations to be solidified into public policy requires some additional, historically based, institutional support. One of the sources of this institutional support is the role of the state government in New York City affairs. Characteristically, some of the most offensive housing policies in New York City have actually been invented in Albany rather than City Hall. The New York State legislature has offered particularly fertile soil for the generation of policies that might not pass muster if decided locally. The legislature has been responsive to the entreaties of well-organized vested or advocacy interests. It is fairly remote from the city press's searching scrutiny. It has the ability to absorb the short term costs of new programs that the city might be unwilling to shoulder—reinforcing the notion that these city/state housing policies are costless.

Not that New York City's own institutions, politicians, or citizens are blameless. Aside from the obvious fact that the offending state legislators, for the most part, represent city constituencies, there are some key, exclusively local, factors at work. The city's governing structure of strong mayor-weak council plus Board of Estimate that prevailed through 1989 depended heavily on the kind of horse trading and deal making that favors short term vested interests over the long term public welfare. The new governmental arrangements for New York City introduced by the 1990 charter may or may not change business as usual in New York.

In any case, New Yorkers are, by and large, unaware that the very city and state housing policies which they often vociferously support work to aggravate their housing woes. The premise of this book is that the underlying dynamics of New York's distressed housing market, the regimen of housing "scarcity by design," can and should be challenged. But to be successfully challenged in the political arena it must be understood. It is our intention to lay out as clearly, accurately and persuasively as possible how the components of New York's housing policy evolved, how they function effectively to sap the housing market's natural vitality, and how they might be changed.

2

All the Wrong People

One of the hit movies of recent years, *Pacific Heights,* is a rent-control horror film in which Michael Keaton plays a deranged but clever tenant bent on terrorizing his yuppie landlords. No matter what he folds, spindles, or otherwise mutilates, they cannot get rid of him. The great mystery about *Pacific Heights* is not its plot, the general outlines of which are perfectly familiar to anyone experienced in the ways of rent control, but its location in San Francisco. This is obviously unrealistic: by all rights this movie belongs in New York City.

By now every New Yorker can reel off rent-control horror stories, and yet rent control retains its political popularity. Why? Surely not just because many influential New Yorkers are tenants paying below-market rents. The more idealistic, and seemingly more persuasive, justification for rent control has been that it makes housing affordable for the poor and working class. Isn't doing right by the poor worth a few horror stories?

But the horror stories, bizarre as they may seem, are not aberrations. The most distressing and consistent reality of rent regulation is what we might call the "all the wrong people" syndrome. With almost faultless precision the rent-regulation system bypasses, or hurts, those it was meant to help, and heaps most of its benefits on relatively privileged New Yorkers. The system does not help the poor; it particularly penalizes new New Yorkers, who have always been vital to the city's economy; and it encourages landlords and tenants alike to behave in ways almost perfectly calculated to tighten the housing market still further and raise rental prices still higher.

There is no trade-off between horror stories and help for the poor; the help never comes, and the horrors remain.

Housing Is Cheap

The abiding sin of rent regulation is that it misallocates resources. It is a truism, for instance, that housing in New York is expensive. But the truism is not true. Housing in New York is cheap, or at least New York has lots of cheap housing, and average prices are reasonable. The problem is that the wrong people live in that cheap housing, while many others are stuck in housing they cannot really afford.

In the last year for which data is available (1987), the median price *including utilities* for all apartments in the city was $395 per month, and fewer than 29 percent of all apartments rented for more than $500 per month. Only 8 percent of all units rented for more than $750 per month. Nor have prices increased disproportionately in recent years. Allowing for inflation, apartments in the New York City are only 12 percent more expensive today than they were fifteen years ago. While the median rent rose 131 percent between 1975–1987, from $171 to $395, consumer prices in general rose 105 percent. Manhattan is the most expensive borough with a median rent of $408 and the Bronx the cheapest at $359, but this modest difference hardly captures the differences in quality and accessibility that characterize apartments in the two boroughs (Stegman, 1982, 1988).

So much for the good news. The bad news is that after years of rent regulation, rents in New York bear little relation to a tenant's ability to pay.

The best test of the relationship between housing costs and ability to pay is the rent-income ratio. For the city overall, the median rent of $395 bears a healthy relation to the median household income (in 1987) of all renters, $16,000, yielding a rent-income ratio of .296 (Stegman, 1988). Theoretically, then, the typical family in New York should be spending 30 percent of its income on rent, within the 25–30 percent guidelines specified by home economists and federal housing officials. However, this statistical artifact—the median rent divided by the median income—would be an accurate picture of the city's housing market only if the rich were paying high rents and the poor low ones. That is not the case. The well-to-do, the great beneficiaries of rent regulation, mostly pay far less than 29 percent of their income for rent, while the poor are routinely confronted with rents they cannot afford. The city's 1987 Housing and Vacancy Survey examined the relationship of prices to income by dividing the renter population into ten income classes and computing the average rent-income ratio for each class. The results clearly show that rent regulation has failed in its primary mission:

- The typical household in the highest income decile of renters, with a mean income of $62,012, paid an average rent of $672 per month, or 13 percent of its income.
- A typical moderate income household, with a mean income of $22,303, paid a rent of $446, or 24 percent of income.
- A typical lower income household, with a mean income of $14,127, paid an average rent of $338, or 33 percent of income.
- A typical poverty-level household, with a mean income of $5,361, paid a rent of $259, or a backbreaking 58 percent of income (Stegman, 1988).

In other words, while the most affluent class of households in New York had an average income over 12 times the poorest, they paid only two and a half times as much rent. And these averages conceal even more glaring inequities: some affluent families devote less than 5 percent of their income to rent, and many poor ones pay more than 70 percent.

To be sure, nearly everywhere in America the rich spend a smaller percentage of their income on rent than do the poor. But nationally the disparity is somewhat smaller than it is in New York. The important point, however, is not that under rent regulation New York's poor do somewhat worse than the rest of the country, but that they were supposed to do much better. If the net result of rent regulation is to make the rental market harder on the less fortunate, and easier for the rich, why have rent regulation at all?

Because rent regulation helps "all the wrong people," it dispenses its greatest benefits to Manhattanites. Only in Manhattan are regulated rents far below market levels. This is the conclusion of the most recent study to examine the geographical incidence of rent-control benefits, conducted by Henry O. Pollakowski at Harvard's Joint Center for Housing Studies. For the city as a whole, median market rents of all apartments were only 15 percent (or $44) higher than rents for regulated apartments. But in Manhattan's better neighborhoods, rents for unregulated apartments ranged from $368 to $432 higher than comparable regulated rents. Excluding Manhattan, the mean rent-regulation subsidy was actually a negative $9—that is, rent-regulated apartments were, on average, entitled to rents $9 higher than the market price. The price-control windfall is largely a Manhattan—specifically, a Manhattan below 110th Street—phenomenon.

Manhattan, outside of its remaining slums, is largely the redoubt of the well-to-do. The average household income of the Manhattan core in 1987 was $35,000, while that for the rest of the city was under $20,000. Only 13 percent of Manhattan core families were in poverty, compared to 23 percent for the rest of the city, and most of Manhattan's poor were living in the pockets of inferior housing without large rent-control discounts.[1]

Why do wealthy Manhattanites reap most of the benefits of rent regulation?

To begin with, to earn the maximum benefits from New York's rent regulations, it helps to occupy an apartment for a long time (because landlords are permitted to raise rents more than usual when an apartment becomes vacant). Affluent professionals have greater job stability and can, in any case, manage to fake their continued occupancy (in order to sublet) when they must move. Also, influence or good connections are helpful in the search for a desirable rent-regulated apartment. The result, as New York City developer Seymour Durst puts it, is that "We've got plenty of low-income housing in New York. We've just got upper-income people living in it."

The Young and the Rentless

That rent control helps the rich rather than the poor is the greatest perversity of the system, but not necessarily the one most damaging to the city's economy or its future. The vitality of New York has always depended very substantially on newcomers, not only immigrants from overseas, but talented people from around the country who are attracted to New York by its great professional opportunities. As the nation shifts to an information economy, and human capital becomes the key factor in production, it becomes ever more important to keep New York a Mecca for new talent. Rent regulation, however, is almost perfectly designed to punish newcomers.

Rent regulation has kept vacancy rates low and housing scarce. So new New Yorkers have a choice between paying exorbitant rents for scarce (by national standards) unregulated apartments, or entering the frantic competition for even scarcer regulated apartments. And, as the young searchers soon learn, a controlled apartments may cost a new tenant a great deal more than the landlord gets in rent.

When Elizabeth Green,[2] a 24-year-old secretary, moved to New York City, she knew that that living costs were high, but assumed that she could find an apartment for $500—much more than what she was used to. What Elizabeth found, like many other New Yorkers, is that $500 doesn't rent an apartment in Manhattan any bigger than a closet.

"When I came from Ohio," Elizabeth recounts, "I expected my costs to be double, which they basically are. Food is double. My salary is double. But my rent is over three times what I had paid before." She pays $495 for her share of an apartment on East 91st Street, but for her, the barrier to living here is more than just $500 a month rent.

"I went to a roommate service. Their fee was $250 to start, including a membership of $35 and two payments of $62.50 after they placed me. Then there was the security deposit, and the first month's rent. So, it cost me about $1,500 just to move in."

The situation is even worse for those young people who, unlike Elizabeth, place a premium on privacy and therefore aspire, like many young Muscovites, to apartments of their own. Available studio apartments in Manhattan fetch between $600 and $900 a month; one bedrooms in safe neighborhoods go for $1,000 and up, while two bedrooms can rarely be found for under $1,500. This is at least twice what one would have to pay for comparable shelter in most other major U.S. cities, even such high-demand ones as San Francisco or Washington, D.C. (Prices have recently softened a bit, but not much, and in any event a major recession is a high price to pay for a slightly less overpriced rental market.)

There is an additional cost of finding an apartment in Manhattan: the broker's fee. Because so few apartments are available, a broker is usually needed to get up-to-date information on all but the least desirable listings. Since a broker's fee (which in some cases includes an illegal kickback to the landlord) runs about 15 percent of the first year's rent, prospective New Yorkers must expect to pay another $2,000 up front.

Sublets, particularly of regulated apartments, often carry a similar cost: "key money," the additional cash fee the new tenant must pay the old tenant for the deal. One new Manhattanite recently told us a classic story: a sublet was available on the Upper East Side for the legal limit of 10 percent above the regulated rent, or about 60 percent of the market price. The catch? The winning applicant would not only have to pay a year's rent in advance, but (in place of key money) would have to buy a $25,000 painting from the legal tenant, an artist.

Add in the usual security deposit of one to two months and the first month's rent, and moving into an apartment can easily cost a new New Yorker $5,000. Five thousand dollars is a major hurdle for many prospective (and even longtime) New Yorkers. How many young workers are eager to move to New York with all its taxes, crime, and congestion, knowing that they will have to come up with $5,000 just to move in?

In the Warehouse

As Moscow shoppers know, the worst result of price controls is scarcity, which New York's housing market has in abundance. The best overall measure of the scarcity of housing is the vacancy rate. The official vacancy rate of New York's rental housing—as represented by the most recent city-commissioned Housing and Vacancy Survey—is 2.46 percent, the lowest among major U.S. cities.[3] The average vacancy rate for all U.S. cities is 5.7 percent, according to the U.S. Commerce Department's most recent American Housing Survey for the United States. Chicago, so frequently compared to New York, had a vacancy rate three times higher (7.5 percent).

The official vacancy rate does not tell the whole story. That statistic is based on the number of apartments that are vacant and available for rent. Oddly enough, despite a tight housing market, New York has just as many apartments that are vacant but *unavailable for rent.*

Why are so many unoccupied apartments kept off the rental mar-

Table 2.1.   Vacant apartments in New York City, 1987

Vacant and available for rent	47,500
Vacant but not for rent	50,300
Total vacant units	138,600

Source: Stegman, 1988.

ket? Some are dilapidated or in abandoned or tax foreclosed buildings, and hardly qualify as housing. But a fairly large number— 53,000 or 3.0 percent of all rental housing units—are perfectly habitable, if not downright desirable (Stegman, 1988).[4] Roughly half of these apartments are really already en route to occupancy, with executed leases or renovations in progress, and they should be counted in the available category.[5] But the other 26,000 apartments are unavailable for two reasons: their out-of-town tenants are holding them for occasional use, or their landlords are "warehousing" them, keeping them vacant for a future co-op conversion or some other deal more attractive than rent-regulated apartments. If all currently unoccupied apartments were put on the rental market, New York's vacancy rate would rise almost to the national average. In other words, much, if not most, of New York's housing crunch is caused by landlords and tenants who keep existing, unoccupied housing off the rental market.

Landlords and tenants in New York keep housing off the market because rent regulation makes it attractive to do so. Out-of-town tenants can afford to keep "pied-à-terres" only because rent regulation makes them so cheap. Surely the purpose of rent regulation was not to provide people with country or retirement homes a comfortable urban retreat. Likewise, warehousing apartments is extremely expensive. Only the truly awful option of renting at far below market to tenants who may never leave drives landlords to the extreme

Table 2.2.   Two measures of New York City's vacant rate, 1987
      (percentages)

Rental units (available vacancies)	2.46
Rental units (all vacancies)	5.06

Source: Stegman, 1988.

of not renting their apartments at all. Once again, rent regulation makes "all the wrong people" do "all the wrong things."

House Wrecking

In 1939, three years before rent control was introduced, Tony Nuzzo's[6] father managed to buy a five-story apartment building on Mott Street in Chinatown. Tony and his wife have been managing the building for his family since 1982. Even though the building is located in a prime location, they are losing money daily and may have to walk away from it.

"We have 35 apartments in the building, totalling 120 rooms," he explains. "Twenty-two out of 35 apartments have rents of $100 or less per month, with the highest rent being $400 and the lowest, $41.25 for a three-room apartment."

With such low rents, the 3 percent annual increase allowed by rent control does little to improve the profitability of Tony's building. With inflation running over 4 percent, New York City's price regulation system insures that this "greedy landlord" cannot possibly make money.

Tony works during the day as a steelworker and moonlights as a boiler repairman, in addition to working on the boiler in his own building. One of his greatest complaints, understandably, is the high income level of the tenants in his building compared to the rents they pay.

"I have one tenant who's a union electrician, which means he's making at least $20 an hour. His wife and his daughter work, and his rent is 55 dollars and 19 cents. I mean, he's a nice guy and everything, but if I even try to raise his rent six cents a month, I would get such a squawk."

There are two ways Tony can avoid losing his building and maybe even make money on it. The current tenants can move out or die, allowing Tony to raise the rents to market levels (after which they will be governed by rent stabilization), or he can take the building co-op. But most rent-controlled tenants are very slow to leave. The system thus gives Tony enormous incentives to drive his tenants out of the building by cutting services or even by active harassment. Some landlords take that course, but Tony refuses to sink to that level. Instead he has tried to buy out his tenants, but rent control gives them a deal Tony cannot beat.

"I offered them $20,000 each. I didn't have it, but I offered it to them. They turned me down. If they had to go find a building on the open market at $1,000 a month, that would last them less than two years. I approached them about converting to condos or co-ops. But who would give you an insider price of $40,000 when they are paying $40 or $60 a month rent? That's almost 100 years of rent. This situation is impossible."

Tony's other option, which he also resists, but which history suggests will be forced on him, is to cut corners on maintenance in the hope his bank account will outlive his tenants. Thousands of small landlords like Tony, the sort of people who for generations were the bulwark of New York's housing stock, have done exactly that: again, the wrong people are forced to do the wrong thing.

As a result, New York's housing stock is in much worse shape than housing in other U.S. cities, large or small. The federal government's American Housing Survey shows that New York City comes off badly under virtually every measure of housing quality, compared with cities in general and even with Chicago, another big city with an old housing stock and an underclass population. On every index of housing condition—all of which are related to maintenance—New York fares miserably. Twice as many apartments in New York have cracked walls, broken plaster, holes in the roof, and exposed wiring than in other American cities. A quarter of New York apartments

Table 2.3. Measures of rental housing quality, 1987 (percentages)

Unit problems	New York	Chicago	All U.S. cities
Large wall cracks and holes	22.6	14.8	13.2
Broken plaster	16.7	10.0	8.0
Peeling paint	22.7	11.8	9.7
Holes in floors	9.7	5.2	4.7
Leaking roofs	14.0	9.6	9.3
Exposed wiring	5.8	3.3	3.8
Broken toilets	5.6	2.2	4.2
Broken heating systems	26.1	8.6	9.2

Source: U.S. Department of Housing and Urban Development and U.S. Bureau of the Census, *Annual Housing Survey,* 1987.

Table 2.4. Measures of owner-occupied housing quality, 1987 (percentages)

Unit problems	New York	Chicago	All U.S. cities
Large wall cracks and holes	6.1	4.6	3.9
Broken plaster	3.9	2.7	2.8
Peeling paint	5.2	3.5	3.3
Holes in floors	1.2	0.8	0.9
Leaking roofs	5.9	6.2	6.0
Exposed wiring	1.3	1.2	1.5
Broken toilets	1.6	0.1	2.0
Broken heating systems	7.5	4.4	3.8

Source: U.S. Department of Housing and Urban Development and U.S. Bureau of the Census, *Annual Housing Survey*, 1987.

have broken heating systems, compared with less than 10 percent in other American cities. Even compared to Chicago, New York's rental housing is poorly maintained.

The case that rent regulation is corroding New York's housing stock is bolstered by data for owner-occupied housing, for which the differences between New York and other cities are much less than for rental units. In fact, on three of the eight indexes of owner-occupied housing, New York shows up better than the other cities. In all cities owner-occupied housing is better maintained than the rental stock, but when rent regulations are imposed the discrepancies become much larger.

New York Is Losing More Housing Than It Builds

The low vacancy rates afflicting New York's rental housing are the product of numerous factors, including the hoarding of apartments by tenants and landlords, and the unwillingness of tenants to relinquish rent-controlled bargains. But the factor that most exacerbates the scarcity of housing in New York is the dwindling amount of new housing being built, especially rental housing.

The pattern of new housing construction over the years has been erratic, waxing and waning with economic conditions, of course, and with interruptions occasioned by war. Yet the housing construction rate in New York City from 1981 to 1986, a period of prosperity and economic and population growth, was 30 percent lower than

Table 2.5. New housing production rates, 1981–86 (percentages)

Dallas	23.16
Los Angeles	7.14
Atlanta	3.77
Boston	2.96
New York	2.02
Chicago	1.60
Pittsburgh	1.49
Philadelphia	1.33
Washington	1.16
Detroit	0.74

Sources: Base-year inventory: U.S. Census Bureau, 1980; annual production figures: U.S. Bureau of the Census, Current Construction Reports, "Housing Units Authorized by Building Permits," 1981–86.

that prevailing in the middle of the Great Depression, when the city was losing both people and jobs. Only during the Second World War, when all non-military efforts had ground to a halt, did New York build less than it did during the economic expansion of the 1980s.

Looking at new housing construction in a comparative perspective, we find that New York lags behind most other large U.S. cities, many of which have suffered population job losses during the time that New York has seen population and job gains. Why is New York, with its severe housing shortage, incapable of building new housing at a rate closer to that of cities such as Dallas or Los Angeles, which have no shortage at all? The answer constitutes the major burden of the rest of this book.

3

The Price of Cheating the Market

Market pricing is the only workable and humane way to allocate consumer goods, including housing. New York City's attempts to cheat the market—through rent regulation, tenure and lease succession rules, warehousing, and other controls—have caused distortions in the housing supply. Tenants move less, buildings deteriorate, property values fall, and construction of new housing is largely restricted to luxury units. The net result of these distortions is a worsening of the very situation which proponents of rent regulation intend to remedy: a scarcity of available housing for low and middle income New Yorkers.

The Role of Prices in a Simple Market

Consider, for a moment, the role of prices in a far simpler market than the housing market. In this simple, perhaps far too obvious example, we can see clearly the effects of attempting to cheat the market pricing mechanism.

Let's suppose that an entrepreneur opens the first grocery store in a small town, and that he can make a good profit, recoup his capital investment, cover the cost of supplies, pay the rent, and give himself a handsome salary, by selling his food at very low prices. His prices are so cheap, in fact, that every afternoon the town lines up outside his store. Within a few hours his stock is exhausted, and half the customers go home disappointed.

The next week, the grocer stocks more food but doubles his prices. The line of customers dwindles to two or three at any given time. In the meantime, both the profitability and the high demand of the grocery business is apparent to other budding entrepreneurs. One of these opens a second grocery store down the street, and prices the food more cheaply. The first shop then lowers its prices as well. Now, at least for the time being, we would have an equilibrium.

In other words, if the price of a good or service is too low, too many customers will be chasing too few items, with products going to the customers who are lucky enough to be in the right place at the right time, or to customers patient enough to arrive early and wait long stretches in line. If the price is too low, there will also be too little of the product being produced (and ultimately, consumed). Yet if the price is too high, customers will vanish, eliminating the profitability of supplying the good, leaving a lot of product left over and unsold. Under such conditions of free exchange, there will be an optimal level of each good or service produced and an optimal distribution of the good among potential customers.

The Temptation to Cheat the Market

Some townspeople might argue that food is so essential that every resident should be able to purchase a "minimum" amount of food each week. They might say that only at "fair" prices would that level of consumption be possible, and might pass a law to set maximum legal prices on food.

Two things might result from this price ceiling. First, selling food at lower prices might no longer be profitable. The town's grocery stores might shut down, and local residents might not be able to purchase this "essential" good at all. Second, if selling food at lower prices were still profitable, the shops would stay in business, but other unfortunate things might happen. Because demand would rise with the lower price, there could well be long lines each day (as in the period before the second shop opened up). People might have to wait hours in line for the privilege of buying the small amount of available food.

Another problem would be the quality of food and service. Confronted with endless lines and a captive market, retailers would start buying cheaper grades of food. Having a captive market, grocers could let their stores run down and behave less politely to their customers. Gradually, the decline in quality and the long queues might provoke public outrage; the local newspaper and some politicians might maintain that the food business could not be safely left in the private sector's hands, and that, for the sake of the "public good," the town itself must get into the food business. The public grocery store must sell food at "affordable" prices, and use tax revenues to make up for any consequent losses to the business. But not to worry, the townspeople would be assured: the tax cost would be very small, because public enterprises are freed from the need to make a profit, and the new public shop would be in a position to undercut the prices of the private food stores.

If the town-operated store were fairly well run, private grocers would be forced out of business. As a result, the public store would have to expand to keep up with demand, but might find it difficult to do so—especially since increased volume would increase any losses caused by selling food at artificially low prices. And over time the wholesale price of food, and of all other consumer items, would rise; but since the town shop would be constrained by political pressure from raising its prices, its losses—and, therefore, the town's tax levy contribution—would also rise. Homes with more mouths to feed might pay less in taxes than they receive through the food subsidy; families that eat less might pay more in taxes than they get back, and would thus be subsidizing their hungrier neighbors. Even more distressing, there would be endless wrangling each year during town meetings about the "fair price" of food.

If, on the other hand, the public grocery store were badly run, townspeople would increasingly patronize the private stores, even paying a premium for privilege, and the public store would lose its clientele. By rights the public store should go out of business, but it probably would not, despite the dearth of customers, because its employees would pressure town officials to keep their jobs.

Apartments Are Like Groceries

Even those who accept the validity of applying market economics to the sale of groceries may reject its application to rental housing, believing that groceries are private consumer goods and apartments are not. But *housing is a private good*. Most housing is produced by the private sector—even in New York—unlike, say, education, street sweeping, or fire and police protection. In the United States as a whole, with a housing inventory of 102 million units, only 1.45 million dwellings, or 1.5 percent, are owned, operated or subsidized by public agencies.[1] In New York, where the percentage is the highest in the nation, 166,000 public housing apartments (those owned by the New York City Housing Authority) amount to only 5.9 percent of the city's housing inventory. To be sure, tens of thousands of additional apartments are under temporary city ownership because of tax foreclosure, and thousands of apartments were built with government subsidies funded by the federal, state, or city governments. But all of these units were built, owned, and operated initially by private developers. Nevertheless, including this inventory still makes public housing only 14.2 percent of the city's stock, leaving 85.8 percent of New York City's housing privately owned and privately managed.

Furthermore, *housing is a consumer good.* One of the most persistent justifications for government intervention in housing markets is that housing is decidedly *not* a consumer good, but a necessity. This formulation is a non sequitur. The "essentialness" of a good, whatever that may mean, does not put it outside the realm of consumer goods. Indeed, many other essential goods such as food and clothing are recognized as consumer goods.

How do we recognize a consumer good? We do so mainly by distinguishing it from its non-consumer counterparts: "merit goods" and "public" goods. A "merit" good is one which society at large subsidizes so that its citizens consume it in considerably larger quantities than they would under normal market conditions, following the rationale that society stands to gain more than the consumer. The premier merit good is education, especially elementary and secondary. Children often do not like school, and if they had to pay for it, many parents would not like it much either. In fact, few economists argue that we would have universal schooling without public compulsion and financing. Yet the requirements of citizenship and the labor force demand a well-educated population, and so education has become a merit good.

"Public" goods are ones whose societal benefit is overwhelming, but so diffuse that there is no effective way to charge consumers a "price" at the point of consumption. The premier public good is national defense. There is no way of gauging how much benefit each American family receives from the maintenance of a standing army, a fleet of warships, or a stockpile of nuclear missiles. Nor is there any way of stopping someone who does not pay for defense from not enjoying its protection. No private entrepreneur or group of entrepreneurs can be expected to install and operate a defense system on these terms. Under the circumstances, the government must produce the good, or it will not be produced at all.

But it can be demonstrated that housing is neither a public good nor a merit good. The public good argument can be dismissed easily. The benefits of housing are discrete, accruing to individual households, and there is no difficulty in charging "admission" to housing benefits. The merit good argument takes somewhat more effort to refute. Housing reformers have long argued that inadequate housing, and slums harm not only slum dwellers but society at large. If such a case could be made, then housing might be a merit good. But the case has grown weaker and weaker over the years because the overall condition of housing has greatly improved, through private initiatives and the supposed connection between bad housing and various societal harms has been impossible to document. Clearly, the benefits of good housing accrue overwhelmingly to the housed.

Cheating the Housing Market

Turning to the real world of housing in New York, we confront many aspects of our grocery-store model. All the harms that would occur by politicizing the retail food business do, in fact, occur as a result of the government's ongoing intervention in the housing business. The key factor in both cases is the *destruction of the necessary role to be played by market prices.*

The one characteristic that truly distinguishes housing from food is durability, and it is durability that has made rental housing so vulnerable to price controls. Perishable goods like food will quickly vanish under a rigid system of price controls, but as a durable and immobile good, the existing supply of rental housing will remain standing for a considerable time after controls have been imposed.

This durability only masks the true shortage that is taking place beneath the surface. The principal surface manifestations of the shortage in housing are increasing deterioration, declining vacancy rates, and, in extreme cases, abandonment.

The best-known instances of interventionism in New York City's housing market are rent control and rent stabilization. But price-fixing is only the tip of the regulatory iceberg. There is also the concept of *tenure*—the condition under which a tenant may remain in possession of an apartment. (For an expanded discussion of tenure rights and lease succession, see Appendix A.) In an unregulated market, the expiration of a lease permits both landlords and tenants to renegotiate terms. And in the absence of a new agreement, the landlord would be free not to renew the lease and force the tenant to move. Any politically effective form of rent regulation, by contrast, will have tenure rules that, in effect, give tenants unlimited occupancy rights. Under New York's rent-regulation program, tenants have statutory leases, meaning that they can stay forever if they wish without a signed lease. Under rent stabilization, tenants are eligible for an endless succession of automatic lease renewals, which amount to the same thing.

One would expect that even under tenant-favoring tenure rules, landlords might regain possession of their apartments in the event of blatant lease violations such as not paying rent, or when a tenant moves or dies. In New York, this is not the case. While nonpayment of rent or damage to premises are grounds for lease termination in most cities around the country, New York City's courts will often rule in favor of the tenants if partial rent payments are made or if the building has some outstanding code violations.

Another explosive issue between tenants and landlords is *lease succession rights*—the right of a tenant to pass on a lease to his descendants. Lease succession is currently a murky area of the law. State courts have issued conflicting opinions about which family members or acquaintances may inherit an apartment, and the state legislature is expected to make further changes in the years ahead.

Under one interpretation of the law, a tenant's immediate relatives are always entitled to a lease renewal under the same terms as the deceased, provided they can prove joint occupancy of the apartment. Other judges have extended succession rights to roommates and more distant relatives. In effect, these extended tenure rights represent a partial transfer of the ownership of the apartment from the landlord to the tenant and are accordingly capitalized in a further diminution of its market value.

The price of housing in the city has been further distorted by New York State's condo/cooperative-conversion rules and the city's recently overturned SRO (single room occupancy) moratorium. The condo/co-op-conversion limitations attempt to seal off one of the remaining routes that building landlords have to escape rent regulations. The SRO moratorium tried to prohibit the landlords of single-room-occupancy hotels from closing, demolishing, or renovating their buildings, so that the city could enlist the SROs in its battle against homelessness.

Because of the city's severe housing crisis, consumer activists have also proposed that the city ban warehousing, the landlord's practice of keeping vacant units off the market. (Absentee tenants who keep vacant apartments off the market are not considered to be warehousing.) The proposed ban would restrict the number of apartments in a rental building that a landlord can keep vacant, even if the vacancies result naturally within the present framework of tenure rights.

In each case, regulations attempt to block an end-run around political attempts to cheat the market. The net effect of these regulations is a distorted market, which benefits least of all those who are supposed to be helped by the regulations imposed.

Lower Property Values

Since anything that affects the rate of return of an asset will raise or lower its value, potential investors in rental properties must factor in the cost of rent regulation. Suppose, for instance, that the total rent roll for an apartment house is reduced in half by a new set of rent regulations. One would expect the value of the building to fall dramatically. Assuming that the building's expenses are constant, a reduction in the building's rent roll will lead to a more than proportionate reduction in its operating profit or net cash flow—the basis of the building's value—and might even make it negative. On the day the rent regulations are imposed, the building's value will have fallen.

The importance of this phenomenon is that potential investors and landlords learn from past experience that their investment will likely suffer unexpected capital losses from increased regulation.

Since "capital is shy," as Adam Smith noted long ago, the expectation of loss causes investors to undertake only those projects which promise above-average or otherwise compensatory rates of return.

Furthermore, because the prices of construction materials—bricks, lumber, roofing, skilled labor, and so on—are set in competitive markets and *cannot* be discounted, new housing production will decline. This drives up the cost of new housing and increases rents. Each control is reflected in apartment purchase prices, because the return for owning a New York City rental building must compete with alternative investments a purchaser might make. Potential landlords must recognize that below-market rents may continue indefinitely. Given the vagaries of the rent-setting mechanism, the quixotic response of the housing bureaucracy and the judiciary, and the uncertainty of consumer behavior regarding lease renewal and succession, the buyer of rental property must demand a further discount in the purchase price to compensate for the risks he may bear of further regulatory confiscations.

Adaptations of Consumers and Suppliers

Economists and others commonly assert that rent regulation and its companion legislation are harmful because they exacerbate housing scarcity—the very phenomenon they are meant to eradicate. That this should be so is evident when we consider the adaptive behavior of consumers and landlords. The principal adaptations of *consumers* in a regulated housing market involve not moving as often as they would under normal market conditions, and settling for a level of housing quality, as measured in amenity or dwelling size, below the level they would prefer under normal market conditions. The principal adaptive behavior of *suppliers* in a regulated market involve allowing properties to deteriorate, and not building as much new housing.

Let's consider each of these adaptive behaviors in turn.

When Tenants Don't Move

The tendency of consumers in a regulated market to move less often than they would in a free market obviously exacerbates housing scarcity. It does not take much of a reduction in tenant mobility, as measured by the average length of tenure (the number of years that a typical tenant has remained in the same apartment) to devastate the housing stock.

By analogy, if you are waiting in line at a bridge or turnpike toll plaza, a small reduction in efficiency on the part of the toll taker can enormously increase the queue and the time each motorist waits to resume his journey. The time it takes the toll attendant to process each motorist is roughly equivalent to the time each tenant spends in a typical apartment. If a toll attendant takes just ten seconds longer processing each motorist, the queue and the waiting time can quickly double.

In just this way, a small increase in the average length of tenure in a rental-housing market can greatly exacerbate scarcity and misallocation, even if housing production rates are reasonably high.

There is no question that rent regulation in New York and in all other regulated housing markets reduces tenant mobility (Arthur D. Little, Inc., 1987). Because the benefits of rent regulation accrue to tenants who stay put, and because the benefits grow disproportionately larger the longer one stays put, a great many tenants will stay put.

Older people, especially older singles, are most likely to lengthen their tenures. They are often retired or close to retirement, and are unlikely to change residence in connection with job or career moves. The primary motive for older households to change residence is the reduction in rent from occupying a smaller apartment: As their children grow up and their spouses die, they have less need for additional space. In a normal housing market, this saving would be available to most elderly households because they could reduce their rent, even in the same location, by renting a smaller apartment. Perversely, in a regulated market, the economic logic works just the other way. An elderly person's present apartment will be cheap not because of its size, but because of the years (if not decades) of rent regulation. For the longtime tenant, any other apartment—even a smaller one—will almost certainly cost more.

The relationship between a head of household's age and mobility behavior in a regulated market is not merely a matter of theory or speculation. Data drawn from recent housing surveys in Los Angeles show that older tenants do move less often under rent regulation.

Los Angeles provides a particularly clear picture of rent

regulation's impact on tenant mobility. Rent control was introduced in Los Angeles in a 1978 ordinance resembling a milder version of New York's rent-stabilization system. Surveys on the impact of rent regulation on the Los Angeles housing market were conducted as recently as 1984 and 1987 and as early as 1977, the last year before rent regulation was adopted. The impact of rent regulation on the length of tenure of elderly households (head of household age sixty-two or older) could not be clearer. In 1977, the average older household moved every 7.7 years. By 1987, the average tenure had increased to 11.1 years, an increase of 44 percent (Los Angeles Community Development Department, 1987). This increase occurred in a mere ten years, under a system where the average allowable rent increases exceeded those of New York's stabilized system.

When Properties Deteriorate

Nearly all housing economists agree that one of the most direct consequences of rent regulation is the deterioration of the regulated housing stock (Barreto, 1986; DeSalvo, 1971; Hamilton, et al., and the Urban Institute, 1985; Lett, 1976; Arthur D. Little, Inc., 1986; Lowry, 1985; Moorehouse, 1972; Olson, 1972; Rydell, et al., 1981; Sternlieb, et al., 1975; Downs, 1988). To quote one of the most recent studies of the issue:

> The revenue losses caused by rent regulation offer landlords an incentive to undermaintain their properties . . . the big question is not whether rent control [causes deterioration of housing stock, but] how rapidly it does so. This analysis estimates that deterioration occurs at a modest but meaningful pace: each year, eight percent of the gap between the current level of housing services and the lower level supported by controlled rents is closed by deterioration (Rydell and Neets, 1985, p. 91).

But one need not rely on economic theory for corroboration of this view. A few days spent visiting New York's rent-controlled housing will give one a firsthand, visual experience of the extent of housing deterioration in New York. If this deterioration were confined to apartment houses in the city's poorest neighborhoods, one might not persuasively be able to assign all the blame to rent regulation. But this deterioration is readily evident in the *best* neighborhoods of New York, and can be seen in particularly sharp relief when comparing regulated and unregulated apartment houses that stand side by side in such prime neighborhoods as Manhattan's Upper West Side; Forest Hills, Queens; or Riverdale in the Bronx.

The deterioration of regulated housing occurs as a result of the intersection of two key market adaptations to rent regulation. On the demand side, tenants are willing to accept a level of housing quality they would not be willing to endure under market conditions. On the supply side, landlords have far less inclination to maintain their properties adequately. Tenants and landlords are both responding to the notion of the "captive tenant," and the adaptations and trade-offs entailed by the lack of consumer choice.

If a tenant is paying a below-market rent in a tight housing market where other regulated apartments are hard to find or would require some kind of under-the-table payment, he knows that to move is to pay more. Thus, the quid pro quo that rent regulation exacts from the tenant in exchange for paying less-than-market rents is less-than-optimal housing quality. On the other hand, since apartment-house maintenance is costly, and the proper upkeep of prime rental properties is particularly costly, the undermaintenance of regulated apartments and buildings is the landlord's quid pro quo, going a long way toward permitting him to recoup the market-regulated rent gap.

When Builders Don't Build

It is also generally undisputed among housing economists and policy analysts that rent regulation depresses the rate of new housing construction. In New York City this effect has become so strong that virtually no new rental housing is being built by the private sector without sizable subsidization. What may not be entirely clear, however, is why this happens. Proponents of rent regulation are quick to point out that New York's rent-regulation laws *exempt from control new housing that is not subsidized or tax-abated.* Opponents of rent regulation counter with two arguments: that the city and state have broken their no-control promise in the past and might do so in the future, and that new rental development must take advantage of available tax abatement and other subsidies to be affordable.

While not entirely dismissing these arguments, which address housing *supply,* we would like to point to a deeper economic explanation for the chilling impact of rent regulation on new construction—one that looks at the impact of control on the *demand* for new housing.

Essentially, builders don't build in a regulated market because they fear that not enough tenants are out there to rent their new apartments. Most tenants for new apartments must be drawn from the ranks of individuals and families already settled in existing housing. In a healthy, unregulated market, landlords can entice many settled tenants out of their existing apartments into newly built developments by offering them better apartments with state-of-the-art kitchens and baths, luxurious appointments, common recreational facilities, and other features that will persuade these tenants to pay more to get more. But this upgrading is only possible in an unregulated market, where increases in rent are more or less proportional to the increases in quality.

In a regulated market, settled tenants, especially affluent families, are the most likely candidates for trading up in quality. However, because they are paying below-market rents, the premium they must pay for new apartments is seldom worth the improvement in apartment quality. Under these circumstances, relatively few middle and upper middle income tenants are willing to move to newly built apartments, and the market for new construction is thus restricted to affluent newly formed families. Therefore, the exemption of new rental housing from the domain of rent regulation, even if carved in stone, is not by itself enough to encourage a healthy level of new housing construction.

Cheating the Market Is Costly

The microeconomic cost of rent regulation in New York City's housing market is that consumers no longer get what they pay for—some getting more than they deserve, but at least as many getting less. And because consumers perceive that finding a new apartment will cost ever so much more, they lose their ability to discipline landlords who supply inferior housing—the ability to walk away and find better accommodations.

The macroeconomic effects of rent regulation are merely the accumulated result of these microeconomic decisions. The housing stock of the city tends to run down as landlords defer maintenance. Little new housing is built to regenerate the stock. New families are left with meager choices, and either pay inflated prices, or leave the city.

Most important, as we shall see, there are psychological, sociological, and, ultimately, *moral* costs of cheating the market. When the exchange of an essential good, such as housing, is governed by factors other than market pricing—particularly when the price process is politicized—relations between consumers and suppliers, such as tenants and landlords, become strained, hostile, and even violent.

4

A World of Adversaries

The tenant-landlord relation has been called the most difficult personal relationship outside of husband and wife. When rent regulations turn voluntary domestic situations into coercive ones, however, previously strained relations become wholly adversarial. Conflicts between owners and occupants, when not resolved through violence or intimidation, are arbitrated by political appointees whose decisions displease all sides equally, ensuring further dispute. The political decisions are implemented by inefficient and corrupt government bureaucracies, providing an additional incentive to resort to extra-legal means. Despite one side's apparent advantage in size and resources, however, the other side tends to win.

The War Between Tenants and Landlords

Consider some of the measures the city's landlords have taken against tenants, and tenant activists, in recent years. In February 1988, concert violinist and property owner Gregory Gelman hired arsonists to pour 40 gallons of gasoline in the basement and on the roof of his five-story building at 204 Eighth Avenue, near 20th Street, in Manhattan; tenants had not paid rent in two years, and in an attempt to recover part of his original investment, Gelman was seeking to collect on the building's $250,000 insurance policy (*The New York Post*, May 3, 1988). In a similar case, four pipe bombs, with fuses, were found before they could be exploded in the basement of a building at 150 West 77th Street, which was in the middle of a tenant-landlord dispute. In Brooklyn, landlords sometimes attempt to collect back rent by kicking in doors and pulling guns (*The New York Times*, August 18, 1990). There are reports that landlords have even loosed pit bulls in hallways to frighten tenants out of rent-controlled apartments so that rents could be raised (statement of Rose Schuyler, April 12, 1988: RSA files).[1] Tenant activists, who often try to organize "rent strikes," have been assaulted by hired goons with abusive language, screwdrivers, and lead pipes, and in June 1989, the body of tenant activist Bruce Bailey was found in a trash sack in the Bronx. His hands and head had been cut off with a power saw, and though the case remains unsolved as of this writing, detectives have been concentrating on landlords as possible suspects (*Village Voice*, August 8, 1989). Whether or not Bailey's tenant work had anything to with his death, some landlords apparently turned his fate into a warning to other activists. Less than a month after Bailey's death, 70-year-old tenant organizer Sophie Kessler, who lives in an Albanian-owned building in the Pelham Parkway section of the Bronx, received a phone call from a man with an Albanian accent. "Don't hang up on me, bitch," the man reportedly said. "We cut you up and kill you like we do the other man." The Jewish grandmother replied: "You ain't cutting nobody up. I have a loaded gun."

Life can be just as dangerous for the city's landlords. Stephen Stribula, who owned a small building in Manhattan, was stabbed to death in 1986 with a butcher knife by tenant Walter Murphy because of a leaky roof (Joseph Stribula, "Requiem for a Small Landlord," undated memo, RSA files). In 1989, Brooklyn landlady Robin Dunn was shot dead by rent-striking tenants as she tried to collect back rent at 1372 Pacific Street. Another small landlord, Kristju Alexiev, has reported that tenant activists punctured his car tires, stopped up his mother's door-lock and his own mailbox with glue, threw poison on plants in his back yard and in his mother's face ("resulting in a swollen face and requiring medical treatment"), and accused his mother of "stealing toilet paper from housing court" (*Greenpoint Gazette*, January 27, 1987, p. 11). Before he was dismembered by a power saw, tenant activist Bruce Bailey reportedly extorted protection money from landlords including Gilbert Bleeks, owner of a building on 136th and Riverside Drive, who alleged in November 1986 that he was forced to pay Bailey $500 to settle a rent strike (Rex Management, 1986.) Tenant activist Alan Flacks (alive at the time of writing) has made a reputation of harassing the owners of 313 West 100th Street, where he lives; in 1983, he warned the building's new owner, Professor William Czander: "You will never move in, you will have to deal with me," and shortly thereafter, Czander began receiving phone calls in the middle of the night, saying: "I will kill you. I will kill your children" (Czander, 1987). By 1988, Czander had sold the building to a Brazilian psychotherapy group, who soon alleged that Flacks had obtained their mailing list and was harassing their clients (Trilogical Enterprises, n.d.). On the Lower East side, tenant activist John Wells placed an illegal wiretap on his landlords, which led to a massive police raid on the owners' apartment after the surveillance reportedly picked up threats by the couple to blow up the rent-striking building (*Greenpoint Gazette*, August 16, 1989). Tenants, too, have apparently been enraged to the point of large-scale sabotage; on March 5, 1990, evicted residents of 13 East 3rd Street showed up at the property with a sledge hammer and a can of kerosene, but were chased away by the owner (*Cooper Square Committee-Tenant Alert*, March 5, 1990).

Violence on both sides has become such a common feature of city life that citizens cannot be assured of the full protection of the law. Marcos Crespo, owner of a six-unit building in Brooklyn, reported in 1986 that tenants had twice threatened to cut his and his sisters' faces and to shoot them when they came to collect back rent, but when Crespo reported these threats to the local police precinct, the police told him there was nothing they could do about "a tenant-landlord matter (Crespo, 1986)."

Why the War Is Fought

In a vicious perversion of the economic doctrine of competition, price controls not only *reduce* competition among producers, but *produce* competition among consumers. As for relations *between* producers and consumers, the natural compact of mutual gain is replaced by a relationship of enforced inequality.

When pricing is unconstrained, both parties to a deal have a variety of first-resort remedies. If, for instance, a landlord charges too much, or maintains his units poorly, tenants can move—or threaten to move—to cheaper or better apartments. If tenants are noisy or destructive, the landlord can refuse to renew their lease. If market conditions change, as they often do, rents and other conditions can be adjusted accordingly. During periods of glut, rents will fall or services improve, while during periods of inflation or shortage, rents will rise or services diminish.

The flux of market forces may occasionally cause distress, but the ramifications of that distress can be accommodated. In small apartment houses, where tenants are likely to know the landlord, rents or maintenance items can be negotiated. In large buildings, tenants might approach the landlord as a delegation to secure relief. Many maintenance issues can also be resolved through tenant efforts, or by negotiating with the building staff—with or without a payment on the side.

Instead of such bilateral agreements, however, two-thirds of New York City's housing stock is overseen by a constellation of political-bureaucratic megastructures. Since this impersonal, governmental apparatus dictates rent agreements and service adjustments affecting millions of citizens—and since the housing agencies may take years to settle individual landlord-tenant disputes—citizens have essentially two choices. They can go outside the law, resorting to threats and acts of violence. Or they can attempt to manipulate the law, forming rival coalitions in the attempt to influence and expedite the political resolution of tenant-landlord disputes.

How the Political War Is Fought

When citizens choose to stay within the law, the city's housing wars are fought by tenant groups, landlord groups, non-profit organizations that habitually take sides, public agencies, legislative committees, and the legislature itself. Leading these groups are tenant activists, landlord activists, bureaucratic activists, and legislative activists. But even with such an array of participants, everything boils down to two antagonistic camps. There is a pro-tenant faction and a pro-landlord faction.

Conflicts between tenants and landlords are resolved by rules for setting allowable rent increases, lease-succession and tenure rights, and other regulations. The rules are made and carried out by arbiters and implementers, for whose allegiance the tenant and landlord groups strenuously contest.

The Arbiters in Albany

The focus of legislative activity at the end of every other or every third state legislative session is the periodic renewal of rent regulations, including New York City's rent control and stabilization. The New York State Assembly, acting principally through the Assembly Housing Committee, takes on the role of champion of the tenants, while the state Senate Housing Committee speaks (by and large) for the landlords.

Because the legislature views rent regulation as a temporary measure, justified by a continuing housing emergency, it continues to pass rent-regulatory legislation with a two- or three-year sunset provision. This has spawned a ritual housing policy minuet in which the extension of rent regulation is by no means the only hotly debated housing topic. Other issues are consistently piggybacked onto the rent-regulation dispute: lease succession, pass-through of landlords' capital improvements, the conditions of co-op/condo conversion, and whether the state will honor previous commitments by allowing subsidized, tax abated middle income housing to return market rents.

The pattern of resolving these issues has become familiar. The Assembly Housing Committee introduces amendments or reformulations of the rent control and collateral-housing laws that represent the tenant position. This agenda includes liberal tenure and lease-succession rules, restrictions on landlord-expense rent pass-throughs for capital improvements, abandoning previous agreements to deregulate middle income subsidized or tax abated projects, and tougher terms for co-op and condo conversion. At the same time, the state Senate Housing Committee proposes legislation reflecting owners' demands: restrictive lease succession, expense-based rent increases, the fulfillment of previous deregulatory commitments, more liberal condo/co-op conversion rules, and gradual deregulation through vacancy decontrol.

The clash of pro-tenant and pro-landlord bills typically ends in a modified form of the status quo, arrived at in the last hours of the legislative session, but only after armies of tenants and landlords have descended on Albany to lobby and to seek media attention. In 1989, for instance, 1,500 unruly landlords marched on the governor's office, only to be told he would not see them; a few weeks later, 1,000 chanting, singing tenants and housing activists staged an impromptu hallway sit-in outside the office of Senate Majority Leader Ralph J. Marino, and taped a rubber lizard to the door of Governor Cuomo's offices, shouting that he deserved a chameleon award for his housing policies (*Newsday*, May 25, 1988).

Playing to the crowd are certain key legislators who promise to battle the "forces of greed," by which they mean the landlords. Some of these legislators—in particular, Brooklyn Assemblyman James Brennan and Manhattan Assemblyman Edward Sullivan—have had close ties with tenant groups, providing them with office space, phones, and even secretarial help (*New York Post*, May 18, 1990).

Behind the scenes, the leaders of the two houses of the legislature—the speaker of the invariably Democratic assembly and the majority leader of the invariably Republican senate—cook up a compromise which, year in and year out, equally dissatisfies both tenants and landlords. "In the last five years, no progress has been made," said Jane Benedict, chairwoman of the Metropolitan Council on Housing, a leading tenant group, in 1989. Over those five years, rent stabilization had been extended, and landlords' allowable increases had not kept pace with inflation, but tenant activists were not satisfied; they wanted the overall level of rents rolled back. The same measures which Jane Benedict found unprogressive from the tenant point of view were denounced by landlord spokesmen as "ruinous" (*Newsday*, June 18, 1988; *New York Post*, June 18, 1988; *New York Daily News*, June 18, 1988).

The Arbiters in New York City

Although the general terms of housing regulation are mandated by the state legislature, the process of actually setting rents in New York City's rental housing market begins each spring with the efforts of landlord and tenant groups to influence the city's Rent Guidelines Board, which meets annually to dictate allowable increases in rents for stabilized apartments.

The board's members, appointed by the mayor, are only occasionally housing specialists. The 1989 lineup was typical: its chairman was a Wall Street broker, and other incumbents included a community activist planner, a bank executive, a college administrator, an investment banker, a legal-services attorney specializing in landlord-tenant issues, two lawyers, and an architect. While most of these individuals had a strong interest and a reasonable grounding in housing issues, none were housing economists, and most viewed their rent-setting responsibilities in terms of an adjudicatory role, trying to balance the claims of tenants and landlords.

As if this balancing act were not an impossible enough task, the board's annual hearings are held in a circus-like atmosphere which renders rational decision-making almost impossible. The June 1990 gathering at Police Headquarters in Manhattan was typical: landlords and tenants drowned each other out with hoots, hollers, hisses, screams, catcalls, and threats. At one point, a shoving match broke out between members of the two groups after several property owners grabbed a banner stating Say NO to Rent Increases from tenants and ripped it up. One tenant yelled at John Gilbert, president of the leading landlord group: "We're going to get you after the show!" The landlords, for their part, paraded through the aisles in modified rabbit costumes, announcing that they were really *kangaroos,* to underscore their concern that the board had become "a kangaroo court."

Such is the process by which the city's Rent Guidelines Board determines the economic fate of nearly one million apartments each year.

The Implementers

While the arbiters are a relatively small band, wielding great power on a limited number of occasions with a few decision "instruments" (legislation, rent guidelines, and so on), the implementers are legion, making very small decisions every day.

At the state level, the principal implementing unit is the New York State Division of Housing and Community Renewal (DHCR), which has been administering both rent control and rent stabilization since 1983. The division is bound by the terms of state housing legislation, but possesses significant rule-setting powers. It must approve landlords' applications for major capital improvements (MCIs), one of few grounds for extra-regulatory rent increases, and must adjudicate thousands of rent-overcharge complaints. The fact that the division is years behind in processing MCI applications keeps many thousands of tenants from having to face annual MCI-based rent increases—and encourages landlords to recoup lost profits by cutting back on services or maintenance, or by forcing tenants out so that rent increases may be allowed.

The municipal counterpart to the division is New York City's Department of Housing Preservation and Development (HPD). Before 1983, the department literally did what the division now does (except for implementing aspects of the rent-stabilization system). Today, the department remains influential by commissioning documents that define the parameters of debate.

One such document is the triennial *Housing and Vacancy Survey.* Under the terms of state legislation extending rent regulation, the city must find periodically that the housing emergency that justified rent control still exists. (A housing emergency is said to exist when the official vacancy rate in the rental sector is less than 5 percent.) In order to document the vacancy rate, the department commissions the U.S. Census Bureau to conduct a comprehensive survey of the housing stock, and selects a housing expert to analyze the bureau's data.

This analysis has traditionally equated the rental vacancy rate with the "availability" of units for rent. The assignment of vacant apartments to the unavailable category, however, depends on the design of the questionnaire and the analysts' subjective evaluation. In recent surveys, for instance, vacant apartments that are actually available for rent have been categorized as unavailable because "they do not afford . . . decent housing" (Stegman, 1985, p. 42).

Besides its role as a mini-ministry of information, the department influences the disposition of the city's large inventory of tax-foreclosed apartment buildings. While this is obviously an important policy issue, it also plays a tangential role in the housing wars. Tenants are determined to keep all tax foreclosed units in the stock of "affordable" housing, while landlords generally favor the reintegration of such buildings into the primary housing market.

The Housing and Preservation Department also administers the city's building code. This is an important battle station, because the building code is the source of so many disputes between tenants and landlords—for example, on issues regarding the proper maintenance of buildings, and the conditions under which landlords may expel tenants who do not pay rent.

As ever when business and politics meet, there is the temptation for bureaucrats to abuse their position and influence, especially in the disbursement of government resources and contracts. The state's housing division, the city's housing department, and government-funded neighborhood-improvement groups have all come under investigation for corruption in recent years. In 1989, as part of a continuing probe into allegations that housing employees routinely steer contractors to certain suppliers, two HPD officials—Joseph Doceti, deputy director of department's capital improvement program, and his aide Russell Fehrenbacher—were arrested for allegedly shaking down private contractors for money in exchange for favorable inspections and confidential information. In 1990, high officials of the state's housing division, including director of administrative services J. Selden Loach, were terminated for "unauthorized activities," and there were reports of more investigations at the division (*New York Daily News*, May 7, 1990).

Abuses have also been uncovered at state-funded groups such as the Fulton Street Improvement Association, a Brooklyn group run by the wife of Jitu Weusi, a Dinkins aide ousted in October 1989 over charges of anti-Semitism. FSIA, which was run out of a corner of the Weusis' co-op grocery store, received about $120,000 from city and state housing agencies between 1986 and 1988 to fix up run-down buildings. After investigating the group's finances, Attorney General Robert Abrams found that over 70 percent of a $45,000 grant to fix up one building could not be accounted for. "They were supposed to paint walls and put up windows. But we went around and found there were no walls, and they hadn't even purchased windows," one source alleged. The state funding was eventually cut off. When asked about the activities of the group, which had held board meetings in his living room, Jitu Weusi replied: "It did not have any links with me. My wife is a liberated woman" (*New York Post*, October 13, 1987).

Tenant Advocacy Groups

Historically, tenant groups have not been grassroots organizations, but rather "action committees" formed by political groups hostile to property rights and market pricing. New York City's first tenant group was organized in 1908 by the Socialist party, and met regularly at party headquarters, watched over by a portrait of Karl Marx (*Harper's Weekly*, January 25, 1925). In the 1930s, tenant organizing passed from Socialists to the American Communists, who led eviction protests and rent strikes. Communist united-front goals appeared behind the blossoming of tenant and consumer councils during 1946, and gave coherence to agitation for rent control throughout the crucial few years following the end of World War Two. These efforts culminated in a January 9, 1947, rally at Albany by 1,800 activists who had been bussed in by the then-Communist-dominated CIO—and led directly to the legislature's decision *not* to lift wartime rent control (Schwarz, 1989).

While it would surely be incorrect to speak of rent regulation as some sort of Communist conspiracy, today's rent regulations and tenant activism *are* a legacy of radical politics. Among tenant groups currently agitating for rent regulation in the city are the Progressive People's Organization, the People's Housing Network, the People's Housing Agenda, and the People's Firehouse, to name just a few. There is also an annual Walk for a People's Housing Policy, sponsored by the Queens Peace and Solidarity Council. The climate of hostility engendered by rent regulation perpetuates conditions of resentment among essentially apolitical residents that can be capitalized on by these political groups.

Most of these organizations are members of the larger umbrella coalition, the Metropolitan Council on Housing, whose ten thousand members pay an average of eight dollars in annual dues. The other major tenant organization is the New York State Tenant and Neighborhood Coalition (NYSTNC), which occupies the same Manhattan office building as the Met Council.

Although NYSTNC is the only tenant organization with a paid lobbyist in Albany, it shares interlocking directorates, personnel, telephone numbers, and addresses with "not for-profit" Met Council member groups, such as People's Firehouse, which are strictly prohibited from lobbying to influence state legislation (undated flyer, RSA files). NYSTNC thus serves as a "shell" or "dummy" unit, allowing state-funded Met Council member-groups to get around the anti-lobbying laws. On April 17, 1986, for instance, NYTSNC/Met Council headquarters hosted a meeting of the Kingsbridge Heights

Neighborhood Improvement Association, whose $38,000-a-year HPD grant proscribed attempts to influence legislation. Yet NYSTNC chairman Bill Rowen told the group: "We need to get out bodies. We're going to Albany to make an impression. We're going to have fun events. Special events to get attention. We will send a message to the Governor and Senate Gallery. All of you must get on a bus" (Kingsbridge Heights Neighborhood Improvement Association, 1986).

NYSTNC's tactics may be questioned on other grounds, such as the group's brazen subordination of factual accuracy to political activism. "We advise *every* tenant to file an overcharge complaint with the state Division of Housing and Community Renewal," stated an August 1988 NYSTNC flyer—the actual rent owed by law apparently not being the issue (NYTSNC, 1988, emphasis added). Members of another NYSTNC-affiliated tenant group lamented in March 1987 that "we got a grant to develop a computer program to help figure out what people owe but it's still a very abstract issue for us. I guess we're getting closer to a day where *we might actually have to* figure out what my people are entitled to" (transcript, Rent Stabilization Association files; emphasis added) In this spirit, NYSTNC organizer David Dower referred in March 1986 to tenant witnesses for the following month's planned invasion of Albany: "*Their testimony doesn't have to be accurate.* Just talk about how this [proposed building] code will get you thrown out of your apartment. Passionately denounce the things that will get you thrown out. If you can sign up, maybe we can get others to testify for you in your place. We'll try it." At the same NYSTNC meeting, People's Firehouse director Felice Jergens went even further: "I don't think we should be rational. The press goes with those who are the loudest, who are thrown out. Why don't we pay actors and children to come out?" (transcript of NYSTNC meeting, March 13, 1986; RSA files; emphasis added).

The People's Firehouse has long employed unconventional methods in its war against the city's landlords. The group itself was formed in November 1975, when former 1960s radicals took over historic Engine Company 212 in Brooklyn and held the fire engine "hostage," blocked the Brooklyn-Queens Expressway with sit-ins, and saved the old firehouse from destruction (*People's Firehouse Bulletin*, September 1985, p. 4). The group's leaders then became unabashed tenant activists in the Greenpoint section of Brooklyn, intriguing by various means to obtain tenant-supplied data on landlords targeted for rent strikes. "Dear Tenant," said one circular, "People's Firehouse, funded by a New York State contract, can install new windows at no cost to the tenant in order to reduce energy consumption. People's Firehouse will send a representative to your apartment to see if you will qualify." When Firehouse representatives arrived for the "weatherization," however, they requested tenants to fill out de-tailed forms, asking for the landlord's name and address (undated circular, RSA files). Soon afterward, People's Firehouse began threat-ening to organize rent strikes against landlords who refused to aban-don their buildings to tenant ownership. "This group is constantly harassing landlords," one owner complained. "It seems their objec-tive is to drag landlords into court for every little thing and cost them legal fees, to have the landlords forced to give up buildings and have the tenants take over so that they can manage the building" (*Greenpoint Gazette*, September 23, 1986, p. 6). In 1984, Firehouse di-rector Jergens began denouncing landlords as "capitalists," and warned building owner Kristju Alexiev that if he did not turn his ownership of his property over to "the working people," he would be "very sorry." When Alexiev refused, People's Firehouse launched a fourteen-month rent strike, ending in a financial loss for Alexiev in the form of five months' rent abatement for what he claimed were tenant-inflicted violations (*Greenpoint Gazette*, January 27, 1987). Eventually, protests from irate landlords resulted in the withdrawal of state funds from People's Firehouse (undated memo, RSA files).

Tenant activism is, in fact, commonly subsidized by city and state government, usually under the aegis of neighborhood improvement. Among the more prominent of such organizations currently operat-ing is the Association for Neighborhood and Housing Development, headed by Bonnie Brower, which received $10,000 in 1988 from the State Council on the Arts "to improve New York City's planning, pol-itics, and programs for meeting the housing and neighborhood needs of poor, working, and minority New Yorkers." The Arts Council, which also approved a $20,000 grant for an adulatory documentary about Sandinista leader Omar Cabezas, did not feel compelled to specify what connection the well-known tenant-activist group had with the arts (*New York Post*, March 17, 1988).

Regardless of their funding, however, tenant groups share a dis-taste for property owners, which, at its most extreme, is tinged with revolutionary rhetoric and racial paranoia. "We know there is a master-plan to drive Black people out [of their apartments], put them in more jails and concentration camps,"stated one tenant-group flier, which called for urban guerillas to "liberate more apartments" (undated flyers: RSA files). Tenant organizer Bruce Bailey had a reputation as an anti-Semite for his repeated references to "Jewish landlords" and scathing articles in his union newspaper, *Heights and Valley News* (*New York Daily News*, June 21, 1989). Landlords are usually depicted on tenant group flyers as "fat-cats" with absurdly Semitic noses, the way Jews were caricatured in Germany in the 1930s. Not all tenant activists go so far, of course; few would consider themselves racists, and a number are themselves Jewish. But even among the more respectable activists, it's taken for granted that the profit motive is immoral and that housing is an entitlement, not something that should be entrusted to market pricing. "In what kind of world does landlord greed outweigh the right to a home?" Met Council head Jane Benedict recently asked (Met Council *Tenant*, February 1990, p. 1). As tenant activist Robin McKay explains: "You're dealing with people whose god is money, who put a low value on human life" (*Village Voice*, August 8, 1989, p. 12).

The Landlord Lobby

While the tenant advocacy groups are politically radical and reliant on small donations or state grants, the landlord groups are well-endowed, professionally managed, politically mainstream organizations. The largest and most active of the landlord lobbies is the Rent Stabilization Association (RSA), organized in 1969. Its 24,000 members, owning 920,000 apartments, voluntarily pay the RSA $2.74 per apartment in annual dues, yielding a budget in excess of $2.5 million. Over the short term, RSA fights for higher rent increases before the Rent Guidelines Board. In the longer term, RSA also fights for all the changes in the housing laws and controls that tenant groups oppose. It would like to make it easier to evict troublesome or delinquent tenants, harder to transfer a lease to anyone other than an immediate relative, and easier to withdraw residential properties from the rental housing market and convert them to cooperative ownership.

The RSA is flanked by a variety of landlord advocacy organizations, some more radical and some more conservative. The largest organization on the RSA's "left" or more radical side is the Community Housing Improvement Program (CHIP), founded by landlord William Moses as a splinter group of RSA's smaller and more economically marginal landlords. CHIP has not only been more militant in engaging in the conflicts of the rent-control wars, but has fought other battles as well, especially for the right of a landlord to occupy at least one apartment in his own building.

The landlord organizations, like the tenant groups, are not above the use of questionable tactics to achieve their aims. Private investigators are commonly hired to check whether tenants really live in their rent-regulated apartments, or are simply profiting by subletting the units at market rates (*The New York Times*, May 9, 1988). The groups also cooperate with building owners to investigate "terror tenants" and activists who might have criminal records, or to find "dirt" on them which might be used to gain leverage in a dispute. The landlord organizations are supplied with "fact sheets" containing such information as tenants' work histories and names of their relatives, as well as social security, checking account, Post Federal Credit Union, savings account, car license plate, Con Edison, and Bank of America Card numbers. Some of this information is obtained by rooting through tenant garbage. Property owners have also infiltrated agents into the tenant groups, to record meetings secretly; this allows the landlord lobby to anticipate and counter the strategies of tenant activists (confidential information in possession of the authors).

Some of the owners' "deep cover agents" also provide information which may be shared with state investigative organs. On August 31, 1987, according to one landlord group's intelligence report on "Neighborhood Preservation Committees": "Agent met with confidential source contact in order to discuss investigative priorities regarding the subject organizations and individuals." These subjects included "a pro-tenant lawyer in Brooklyn," as well as "numerous housing and tenant groups," and "various political campaign headquarters." "The source is privy to information, and his support will enable us to utilize this information to our best interests, in a very timely manner" (confidential information).

In sum, the politicization of the price process in New York City's rental housing market brings out the worst on each side. As one small-building owner has lamented, "Both tenants and landlords abuse the system to such a point that it has become lawless" (Undated Housing Court Questionnaire of Norma and Romeo Persuad: RSA files).

The Secret of Their Success

The targets of tenant and landlord advocacy are primarily the arbiter panels such as the New York State legislature and the Rent Guidelines Board, although they also hope to influence the courts, and public opinion generally. Judging by the outcome of specific battles, the tenant groups have been far more successful. Rent guidelines in most years have been held below the level of general inflation, while tenure and succession rules have similarly evolved to tenants' benefit.

There is, in fact, virtually no correlation between the apparent size and power of the tenant groups and their level of influence in the rent-regulation process. Given the apparent imbalance of resources between adversaries, why are the underdogs so successful?

The influence of the tenant organizations rests ultimately on two factors: the forceful and articulate presentation of their agenda by dominant personalities—made as much through the newspapers and television news as on the floors of the decision-making bodies—and the belief, held by politicians and adjudicatory arbiters, that these organizations could mobilize thousands of tenants if challenged. NYSTNC chairman Bill Rowen has described this pressure process as one by which "we can continue to scare [Republican senate leader] Warren Anderson so he keeps throwing something our way" (Kingsbridge Heights Neighborhood Improvement Association, 1986).

Tenant activists like Rowen, moreover, have a fairly narrow agenda: they want people to pay as little as possible for housing. Landlords, by contrast, have a diverse (and often inconsistent) agenda. Many landlords have an immediate stake in the favorable disposition of issues affecting their own—*and only their own*—properties. They may need approval for a new development, a zoning change, an MCI increase, or approval of a co-op conversion plan. Many of the most powerful figures in the industry would rather use their individual and collective political influence to secure favorable incremental decisions affecting their own properties than necessarily to change the entire basis of housing policy and rent control. The focus of debate is thus not *whether* rent-control regulation be continued, but *under what terms* it should be. "Don't worry," tenant leader Bill Rowen recently told his supporters, "the rent laws will always be renewed. They, the landlords, just use this as an opportunity to *weaken* the rent laws" (Kingsbridge Heights Neighborhood Improvement Association, 1986; emphasis added).

The landlords' disunity, and their de facto agreement that the state should be in the rent-fixing business, preclude any effective opposition to regulation. Until such opposition develops, rent regulation will remain. And as long as rent regulation remains, landlord-tenant relations will be politicized, hostile, and sometimes violent.

That New York City's housing market seems likely to remain a world of adversaries, with profits made or lost by lobbying luck, is just one more reason for housing entrepreneurs *not* to invest in new construction—and one more ultimate cause of the city's housing scarcity. As chapter 6 intends to show, however, this scarcity is a result not merely of the present situation, but of regulators' refusal to honor commitments made to landlords and developers in the past.

5

Once Upon a Time

Rent control became a central political issue in New York City and New York State politics early in the twentieth century. Thomas Jefferson's idea of a rural, property-owning society with strict limits on government power was a distant abstraction to immigrants who were struggling to find a job and a home in the New World. The sheer scale of development in Manhattan led to more distant relationships between landlord and tenant, with ever greater numbers of voters who rented relative to those who owned property. As the city expanded, the politics of New York State became increasingly oriented to the needs of city dwellers, 80–90 percent of whom were renters (see Table 5.1 below). Their historical experience as landless immigrants left them with strong animosities against landlords and made them more disposed to redressing their grievances through state and city politics.

Another cause for the politization of rent control was the expansion of government and the inflation that accompanied World War I. The wartime inflation was unexpected coming after a long period of relatively stable prices in the nineteenth century. The rapid rise in prices was especially noticeable in rental housing contracts, where by custom the rent amount is fixed for one or two years and then adjusted by a large amount when the new lease is renegotiated. Because rents did not rise relative to inflation during the term of the lease, the increase in rent thus came all at once and represented a significant portion of the typical consumer's budget.

Indeed, the three times in U.S. history that rent control has been

Table 5.1. Inflation rates during first-generation rent control (percentages)

1914	1.3	1922	−6.3
1915	1.0	1923	1.8
1916	7.6	1924	0.2
1917	17.4	1925	2.5
1918	17.4	1926	1.0
1919	14.9	1927	−1.9
1920	15.8	1928	−1.3
1921	−10.7	1929	0.0

Source: U.S. Bureau of the Census, *Historical Statistics of the United States, Colonial Times to 1970*, p. 211.

introduced or expanded were all times of inflation: the post-World War I inflation, the World War II inflation, and the Vietnam War inflation of the 1970s.

First-Generation Rent Control, 1920–1929

During World War I, rent controls were imposed in Russia, England, France, and in many parts of the United States: Connecticut, Delaware, Maine, Massachusetts, Nevada, and Virginia passed legislation to limit rents for servicemen and their families. In March 1918 Congress passed a national rent-control bill for servicemen, and by June passed a rent-control bill to cover all apartments in Washington, D.C., freezing rent levels in the capital until one year after the conclusion of the war. Congress was concerned that landlords were profiteering at the expense of soldiers and the growing number of government and defense industry workers (*New York Times*, July 28, 1918).

Rent control wasn't implemented in New York until the aftermath of the war. Several bills to encourage lower rents were introduced in the state legislature between 1910 and 1913, each one known by the names of its authors—the Sullivan-Brooks, the Sullivan-Short, and the Salant-Schaap bills. These bills were not actually about rent control. The Salant-Schaap Bill of 1913, for example, merely provided for a referendum to cut the tax rate on improved property, with the expectation that reduced expenses and increased construction would lower rents (*New York Times*, April 7, 1913).

In the state capitol, tenants argued that landlords were "war profiteers" and lobbied for legislation to make excessive rents a crime. Landlords charged that rent increases were reflections of the city's high property taxes and that a cut in the tax rate was needed immediately.

Exacerbating the apartment availability problem was the low level of new construction during the war. Only 40 percent of the normal volume of new housing was being constructed, whereas housing demand for the first quarter of 1919 was estimated at 133 percent of its normal level (*New York Times,* March 31, 1919). Land prices and labor costs were bid up during the war, and while developers were waiting for prices to stabilize, little housing was being built and apartment rents hit extraordinary levels. In his study of housing between 1914 and 1943, Herbert Swan found that several rent indices began rising rapidly during 1917–1918 after three straight years of little or no increases (Swan, 1944). For example, the Bureau of Labor Statistics rent index rose 20 percent between December 1917 and December 1919. The Federal Reserve Bank of New York's index rose 41 percent between May 1917 and May 1920 (ibid.).

Despite the evidence of rising rents, both Governor Al Smith and the Advisory Council of Real Estate Interests, a landlords' lobby, opposed rent control as late as March 1919. As one would expect, the Council did so quite emphatically, denouncing any system of prices other than the free market. Governor Smith, however, simply stated that he favored cooperation more than laws as a way to solve the housing problem and formed a Reconstruction Commission to look into the economy's adjustment to peacetime (*New York Times,* May 17, 1919).

Twelve months later, the governor shifted his position and announced that he, too, was ready to fight profiteering, at least as far as the state constitution would permit. Smith urged that the legislature adopt the recommendations of the Reconstruction Commission, which included the establishment of housing boards in communities with more than 10,000 people, and the enactment of a constitutional amendment permitting an extension of large-scale state credit at low rates to aid construction. (New York State Reconstruction Commission, 1920; at Swan, 1944).

On March 31, 1920, the legislature responded to an emergency message from Governor Smith and passed eleven bills to provide relief to renters and to stop profiteering. Senate Majority Leader Henry J. Welters noted that the constitutionality of the legislation rested upon whether an "emergency" existed and ruled that an emergency did exist, which gave New York State the right to use its police power (Swan, 1944). The most important element in the package permitted tenants to stop paying rent if the amount had been increased by more than 25 percent in any one year. An increase above this amount was deemed "presumptively unjust, unreasonable and oppressive" (ibid., pp. 39–40). Along with the automatic ceiling on rent increases, tenants were given three months to challenge their newly agreed-to rent level in the city's housing court. Not only was a landlord subject to a court-ordered rent rollback, but as Swan noted, "The net result of these provisions was to insure to a new tenant the maintenance of the rent status quo as of three months after the date he moved into the apartment" (ibid.). Even if the tenant didn't challenge his lease in court, the new rent amount would be fixed indefinitely.

The companion bills repealed a law allowing the landlord to collect double rents should the tenant refuse to move following lease expiration, and they allowed the tenant to remain in his apartments for nine additional months at the court's discretion, provided the tenant could prove he tried to find alternative housing. One result of this provision was to extend the renting season well beyond normal September 1 deadline as tenants shopped around, knowing their existing rent level was held in check. Another feature of the legislative package loosened the eviction laws by shifting the burden of proof to the landlord for showing that a tenant was objectionable.

Landlords challenged these new rent laws immediately, and lower court decisions began rolling in one week after the laws were enacted, either limiting the scope of the regulations or inviting a Supreme Court review of rent regulation. In several cases in 1920, for example, Bronx Municipal Court Judge Harry Robitzek granted one-year extensions to tenants who came before his court, and set new rents at 20–25 percent above their March 1919 levels (*New York Times*, April 8, 1920). With inflation running at 15–20 percent annually and many leases running for multiple years, these rulings actually represented rent rollbacks in many cases.

Not all of these decisions were upheld by higher courts. When Municipal Court Judge John R. Davies ordered rebates on all leases signed later than April 1, 1919—one year prior to the passage of rent control—his ruling was struck down by State Supreme Court Justice Irving Lehman, who cited the ex post facto clause of the federal Constitution prohibiting retroactive legislation (*New York Times*, April 20, 1920, and May 30, 1920).

In October 1920, the Supreme Court of the United States agreed to move ahead on their calendar two cases from New York City and Washington, D.C., to test the constitutionality of the rent control laws and was expected to issue a decision the following April (*New York Times*, October 27, 1920).

Much debate preceded the court's decisions. Harold M. Silberman of the Real Estate Investors of New York stated that the rent laws should be struck down on three grounds. First, practical: the litigation required under the laws was straining the solvency of many small owners—between 20–25 percent of all rent payments in the city for October and November 1920 were currently before the courts. Second, constitutional: the rent laws voided private, voluntary contracts in violation of the Constitution's prohibition of impairment of contract. Third, economic: the rent laws discouraged new construction (*New York Times*, November 21, 1920).

Nevertheless, the issue facing the Court was not the wisdom of rent control but its constitutionality. In his earlier decision upholding the law's constitutionality, State Supreme Court Justice Leonard A. Giegerich stated, "Whatever injuries an individual may suffer in the diminution of his property rights are, however, deemed to be made up to him by his sharing in the general benefits which the regulations secure to the community of which he is a member" (*New York Times*, December 7, 1920). Justice Giegerich declared the laws a reasonable police action that did not deprive people of their property without due process of the law.

The Court finally settled the constitutionality of rent control in the landmark case of *Block v. Hirsh*. The plaintiff, Hirsh, was a Washington, D.C., landlord who sought to evict the tenant, Block, at the expiration of his lease. The District of Columbia's rent statute permitted landlords to evict tenants provided that the rental unit would be used by the landlord and his family and that the tenant be given thirty days notice before the eviction. Although Hirsh did plan personal use of the property, he refused to give the statutory thirty days notice. Hirsh claimed that the rent statute authorized the taking of "private property for public use" with compensation, in violation of eminent domain clause of the U.S. Constitution (Epstein, 1988).

In the 5–4 decision, the Court ruled in favor of the defendant Block, with Justice Oliver Wendell Holmes writing the opinion for the majority with the concurrence of Justices Brandeis, Clark, Day, and Pitney. Dissenting were Justices McKenna, White, McReynolds, and Van Devanter (*New York Times*, April 19, 1921). The court upheld the statute, justifying it as "a proper exercise of the police power for 'civilized' societies in wartime conditions." Justice Holmes argued housing was a necessity and determined (implausibly) that the rental housing market in Washington was monopolized by a few landlords (Epstein, 1985). Consequently, Holmes concluded, Congress was perfectly justified in declaring an emergency housing situation and the Court must defer to the will of Congress.

By adopting the housing emergency and police power line of argument, Holmes avoided the issue of whether or not the state had conducted a taking. The *Block v. Hirsh* ruling was further upheld in the New York test case of *Marcus Brown Holding Company v. Feldman*, finally establishing rent control as a legal policy instrument during times of "emergency."

As one might expect, once precedent had been established, state legislators and city officials throughout the country began urging the extension of rent regulation. Rent-control laws were soon passed in Arizona, Illinois, New Jersey, and Oregon, and by the cities of Baltimore, Denver, Jersey City, and Los Angeles. Upon the request of Governor Smith, the New York legislature expanded the rent-control laws to cover all tenants, not just those who signed their leases before the laws were enacted.

New York's rent-control laws were extended in 1922, 1924, 1926, 1927, and 1928, but in successive years they covered an ever smaller segment of the housing stock. Fewer units were covered by regulation and the return of low inflation meant smaller, less objectionable rent increases for unregulated apartments. The 1926 extension initiated a decontrol program by exempting all apartments renting for more than $20 per room. This "luxury decontrol" ceiling was reduced to $15 in 1927 and to $10 in 1928, so that by 1928 only 20 percent of all rental units were covered by controls (Swan, 1944; Tobier and Espejo, 1988). When Governor Smith signed the 1928 partial extension, he called for an end to the city's rent regulations (*New York*

Times, April 7, 1928). On June 1, 1929, New York City's rent-control statutes expired (*New York Times*, June 1, 1929). Several weeks later, New York City Board of Alderman passed a local law to regulate rents (*New York Times*, June 12, 1929). A state court struck down this ordinance, however, on the grounds that the state law preempted the city's on this matter (*New York Times*, November 20, 1929).

One result of the imposition of rent control over the 1920–29 period was an increasing tendency of tenants not to move and a divergence of the rents between new and existing tenants. A 1923 study by the Commission on Housing and Regional Planning found that tenants who moved into their apartment in the last twelve months paid an average 45 percent more in rent than tenants who had lived in an apartment of similar size four to five years earlier (Swan, 1944).

Vacancy rates were abnormally low during the imposition of controls, reaching a low of 0.8 percent in 1924 but gradually rising as the controls were phased out. The Great Depression exacerbated the trend of rising vacancies in the early thirties before the rate stabilized in the 6–8 percent range in the years prior to America's entry in World War II (Block, 1972).

Beyond the economic effects to New York City residents and the housing market of the time, the 1920–29 rent-control program and the landmark *Block v. Hirsh* case set an important legal precedent that increased the power of state and local governments to regulate housing. The importance of the concept of a rental housing emergency, however, has remained a crucial test in the Court's mind for the constitutionality of controls. The Washington, D.C. statute was struck down in 1924 in the case of *Peck v. Fink* on the grounds that a hous-

Table 5.2.   The rise in vacancy rates in multi-family dwellings (percentages)

1924	0.80
1925	2.11
1926	3.46
1927	6.63
1928	7.76
1931	12.02
1934	13.72

Source: Swan, 1944, p. 42.

ing emergency no longer existed, even though the federal statute was not due to expire until 1925. Ultimately, the 1920–29 rent control laws proved to be much less severe than subsequent rent regulations. But while conceding that the controls were a failure, city and state officials no longer felt greatly constrained by the traditional interpretation of the Constitution.

Second-Generation Rent Control

In 1942, Congress passed an Emergency Price Control Act to curb wartime shortages and inflation. Rents were to be frozen at their March 1, 1943, levels for all cities deemed "defense rental areas."[1] This legislation sought to prevent any leakage of economic resources away from the war effort, and because wages and many prices were also controlled, wartime rent controls appeared to cause little specific damage to housing.

After the war ended, the Republicans swept into control of Congress on a platform of freeing the economy from the myriad of wartime controls, which had caused a shortage of housing and other goods. In July 1947, Congress passed, and President Truman reluctantly signed, a bill to lift controls on all wages and most consumer prices, and to decontrol rents for all housing built after February 1, 1947 (The Economist, July 5, 1947; Citizens Housing Council of New York, 1947). Responsibility for enforcement of the remaining rent controls on the "prewar housing" was given to the states and localities. And in its 1949 extension of federal rent controls, Congress gave cities and states the option to decide whether to continue or remove rent control, an option many cities did not welcome (Congressional Quarterly Annual Report 1949). Congressmen from St. Louis, Chicago, and New York City (Jacob Javits and Adam Clayton Powell) spoke of their fears that Republican-controlled legislatures in their states would deny their cities the authority to pass rent-control laws (Block, 1972).

In response, Congress let its final extension run to 1953, giving local governments until July 1 to pass their own local rent-control ordinances. The last major cities to have rent control following the war were Los Angeles (decontrolled in 1950), Chicago (1953), San Francisco (1953), Washington, D.C. (1953), Boston (1955), Baltimore (1956), Philadelphia (1956), Newark (1957), and Honolulu

(1961). By 1961, New York was the only place in the country with rent control (Block, 1972). For this reason, New York's 45-year experience with rent control has been unique in the United States (though, of course, the rent-control systems that are in effect today in many European cities originated in World War I). Only with the onset of the great inflation of the late 1960s and 1970s would rent control be imposed in any state other than New York. Today, only six states and the District of Columbia have rent-control laws. New York, New Jersey, Connecticut, Massachusetts, and California have rent-control statutes covering a large number of cities and towns, and Maryland has rent control only in the D.C. suburb of Takoma Park (HUD, 1991).[2] Sixteen states, largely in the Southeast and Southwest, have state-wide statutes or constitutional amendments that prohibit local imposition of rent control by any municipality.[3]

6

Broken Promises

Advocates of rent regulation often deny that it inhibits new construction or causes scarcity. They argue, correctly, that since existing statutes typically exempt newly built apartment buildings from controls, some other factor must explain the reluctance of builders to invest in rental housing. What rent regulators fail to see is that one of these factors is the developers' expectation of future regulation. The most formidable deterrent to future investment in rental apartments is not so much current law as New York's propensity to change the rules of play when it is politically expedient to do so. Because of the paramount importance of the next election, most politicians heavily discount the future in public policy. This causes investors in real property, who must think in terms of decades, to heavily discount future positive cash flows and long-term capital gains when they have reason to distrust the promises of politicians. This discrepancy in time horizons and visions between politicians and developers has resulted in a series of broken promises and dashed expectations that continues to this day.

The Postwar Betrayal

The most significant example of an intentionally broken promise has been the New York State legislature's repeated pledge not to regulate any apartment buildings constructed in the future. Mindful of the chilling effect that rent regulations would have on future development, the legislature has explicitly exempted all or most prospective construction. However, after enough developers rise to the bait to produce sufficient units to house a substantial political constituency, the government goes back on its word and regulates the housing that was once exempt, all the while promising never to do it again.

This cycle began after federal decontrol of rents in 1949, when the New York State legislature exercised its option to regulate rents by passing the Emergency Housing Act of 1950.[1] To fill the regulatory role that the federal Office of Housing Expediter had played, this legislation created the Temporary State Housing Rent Commission. This extension of wartime regulations into a prosperous peacetime economy constituted the first of betrayal of trust with those who would build or own rental housing.

It also distorted the market. Since the state's rent-control code permitted a standard 15 percent increase whenever a tenant moved out,[2] rents for units with high tenant turnover soon exceeded units with lower turnover. Consequently, in many apartment buildings *the least desirable apartment*, with the highest turnover—the basement apartment or one with the poorest view or lighting—came to have *the highest rent*. Since the more desirable, low turnover apartments had fewer vacancy increases, their rents tended to lag behind the rate of inflation. Finding their rents were falling (after inflation), tenants in these apartments tended not to move out, only reinforcing the distortion of the rent-control legislation.

Despite these distortions, the 1950s were not a terrible time overall for housing in New York City. The city's population was stable, and real income rose. And since it was a period of relatively low inflation, the gap between controlled and uncontrolled rents did not widen too much. Moreover, a massive amount of construction took place; over 300,000 new dwellings were built by 1957. Because the rental housing shortage had substantially eased, the legislature decontrolled luxury apartments renting for more than $5,000 a year (or $416.67 a month).

In addition, 30,000 to 35,000 rent-controlled apartments were vacated every year, thus permitting significant rent increases for the controlled stock. One study found that rents for controlled apartments in New York City rose 40 percent over the decade, whereas rents in other parts of the country rose 25 to 52 percent (Tobier and Roistacher, 1986). And as newly built rental units were kept free of controls, the percentage of apartments under the rent-control system gradually fell. Finally, the rapid expansion of public housing projects and limited-profit housing projects in the postwar years meant that the rent-controlled sector became less and less important. By 1969, only 60 percent of the city's rental apartments were covered by the rent-control laws—the lowest rate since before the war.

The Rent-Stabilization Betrayal

The year 1969 was a watershed for New York City's housing policy. By 1970, the level of rent regulation had gone from its postwar low to an all-time high. The promise of not imposing rent control on postwar apartments proved to be little more than a semantic deception: postwar units, entrepreneurs were told, were not going to be rent-*controlled;* they would merely be *stabilized.* How did this happen?

By the late 1960s, the city had three distinct housing policies: heavy-handed regulation for the 1,267,000 pre-1947 rental units; an unregulated market for the 686,000 dwellings that were either postwar units or had been decontrolled; and a generous tax policy and an unregulated market for the 671,000 owner-occupied units (Marcuse, 1979). Rental housing developers and their mortgagees believed that their postwar properties would be free to compete in the housing marketplace. After all, administration of rent controls had passed from federal to state to city government with relatively little modification. The application of the regulations had been tightened, but over 200,000 units had been removed from their purview and none had been added.

Developer confidence in the early 1960s spurred a rental housing construction boom, one given additional force by the city's adoption of a new and more restrictive zoning law that did not go into effect until 1964, making developers rush to get their projects on line under the old zoning. Of the more than 250,000 new units that were built in this period, over 70 percent were built by the private sector and without subsidy (Tobier and Espejo, 1988). In part owing to this new construction, vacancy rates in the city hit a postwar high of 3.19 percent in 1965: 2 percent in the controlled sector and 5 percent in the uncontrolled sector (Kristof, 1975).

This zoning-induced housing boom, however, was soon followed by a zoning-induced housing bust as the new zoning law took effect,

Table 6.1. New York City's roller-coaster vacancy rates (percentages)

1960	1.81	1978	2.95
1965	3.19	1981	2.13
1968	1.23	1984	2.04
1970	1.50	1987	2.46
1975	2.77		

Source: Stegman, 1987, p. 43.

making apartment house development much more expensive. New housing construction fell from 48,767 per year in 1961–65 to 20,842 in 1966–70, and the vacancy rate fell to a postwar low of 1.23 percent in 1968 (New York City Department of City Planning, 1986). Not surprisingly, rents began to soar.

A growing number of city voters in unregulated apartments, paying much higher rents than tenants in rent-controlled apartments, began demanding extension of rent control to their units. City Rent and Housing Commissioner Frederic S. Berman echoed the sentiments of these renters, alleging that landlords were demanding "rent gouging" increases of 40 to 60 percent in some of the city's 700,000 uncontrolled apartments (*New York Times*, July 22, 1968). Then, in the middle of Governor Rockefeller's 1962 re-election campaign, the state legislature passed an Emergency Housing Act, which shifted management of rent control to the city, a political unit much more dominated by renters.

With the city's enhanced powers to regulate rents, the inflation of the 1960s made pro-tenant legislation irresistible. Mayor Lindsay warned landlords to roll back "excessive" rent increases and accept voluntary rent guidelines within three weeks or face regulation by the city. By February 14th, the Mayor had formed a nine-member Rent Guidelines Board consisting of businessmen, professors, and community leaders to make recommendations for voluntary rent guidelines.

On March 10, the Rent Guidelines Board issued its first guidelines: that owners of the city's 400,000 uncontrolled apartments voluntarily limit themselves to a 15 percent rent increase on two-year leases, and 20 percent for three-year leases; and that tenants should get a credit for any increase above 15 percent agreed to since October 1 (New York City Rent Guidelines Board, 1969).

In the weeks that followed the announcement of the new guide-

Table 6.2. Growth of the rent stabilization program

Year	Prewar units	Postwar units	Total units
1970	—	350,000	350,000
1975	467,000	303,000	770,000
1978	552,000	320,000	872,000
1981	615,000	313,000	928,000
1984	638,000	305,000	943,000
1987	663,000	272,000	935,000

Source: Arthur D. Little, 1985, p. 4; Sternlieb and Hughes, 1976, p. 40. No
statistically valid survey of housing was made between 1970 and 1975, the
period when vacancy decontrol was enforced.

lines, the city council became concerned that the permitted level of
rent increase was too high and that the sanction for not obeying it
was too weak. Some eighteen bills concerning rent control appeared
before the city council (Keating, 1978) and a special committee con-
tended that a lower increase, 4–5 percent, would have been a more
appropriate guideline.

On April 24, 1969, the city council rejected the mayor's voluntary
approach and passed the Rent Stabilization Law of 1969, which ap-
plied to all rental units built between 1947 and 1969 in buildings of
six units or more. As some 350,000 apartment units were initially
stabilized (though the program would later grow to over 900,000
apartments), the state completely reneged on its implied promise
since 1947 to allow postwar housing to remain unregulated.[3]

The Rent Stabilization Law represented a radical change in the
philosophy of rent regulation. Since the city recognized that freezing
the rent level of the uncontrolled apartments would be damaging to
their upkeep, the new legislation provided for annual increases.
However, the method of increase—the decision of a nine-member
mayoral commission—only politicized regulation of the housing
stock even more. While the new program initially covered a smaller
number of apartments than rent control, rent stabilization would
eventually become the dominant regulatory mechanism of the city's
housing stock.

The Vacancy Decontrol Experiment

New York City's overt betrayal of the trust bestowed by Governor
Rockefeller and the state legislature led state officials to question the

city's unrestricted right to regulate rents. Frank Kristof, chief economist with the state Urban Development Corporation, testified before a State Housing Committee in 1969 that the city had suffered dramatic losses of housing units largely due to rent control. Governor Rockefeller's housing commissioner, Charles J. Urstadt, warned in March 1970 that hundreds of additional apartment buildings would be abandoned in the next decade if the rent-control laws were not eased (*New York Times*, March 5, 1970).

To arrest this pattern of housing abandonment, Governor Rockefeller presented a legislative package in April 1971 which decontrolled all apartments that were vacated and changed tenants on or after June 30, 1971. And, to prohibit a return of more stringent forms of rent control, the legislature passed several bills, popularly known as the Urstadt Laws. Still in force today, these bills prevent the city from enacting any law or regulation that is more stringent or restrictive than those that were in effect on July 1, 1971.

In addition to the rent-deregulation package, Governor Rockefeller and the legislature were determined to spur new housing production and hoped to accomplish this through legislation for a new city housing-subsidy program known as the Section 421 Partial Tax Exemption Program. Designed to reduce the burden of New York City's high property tax rates, Section 421(a) phased in the imposition of full real estate taxes on new apartment buildings over a period of 10 years.

The 1971 amendments brought a new sense of optimism to those who would build, buy, or finance rental housing. The state had taken the pledge and committed itself to phasing out rent laws—through decontrol of the existing stock, and by not regulating new buildings unless they received tax benefits (and even then, only for a limited time). Above all, the Urstadt Laws prevented the city, which then administered controls, from thwarting the will of Albany.

The Emergency Tenant Protection Act

The vacancy decontrol experiment of 1971–73 was derailed by Governor Rockefeller's resignation in December 1973. Malcolm Wilson, Rockefeller's successor, was a conservative suburban politician without the immense personal fortune of a Rockefeller or a solid political constituency of his own. He was heading a Republican ticket in the aftermath of the Watergate scandal in a predominantly Democratic state, and as Rockefeller's lieutenant governor, he was not very well known and had not developed much electoral support. He attempted to build a constituency by proposing a pro-tenant bill, known as the Emergency Tenant Protection Act (ETPA) of 1974, that would effectively repeal vacancy decontrol. The final version of ETPA was written by conservative Republicans in the legislature and adopted on May 16, 1974.

The principal result of the ETPA was to regulate all apartments in buildings of six or more units built between 1969 and 1974 and to reregulate all apartments in the same-size buildings that had previously been vacancy-decontrolled.[4] ETPA also abrogated the agreement that existing 421(a) buildings containing six or more units would be free from regulation after ten years.

Owners who were contemplating the construction of new buildings after enactment were assured that their apartments would not be regulated, but this time the promise had a new wrinkle. Newly constructed apartment buildings would not be subject to rent fixing *unless* they were receiving some form of tax exemption or abatement (such as was readily available under Section 421(a) and J-51 tax abatement programs). To encourage participation in these programs, the rent-stabilization law governed only those properties that were receiving tax benefits. Deregulation was supposed to occur when the phase-in expired and full taxes were being paid.

The only portion of the 1971 liberalizations to remain intact after 1974 were the Urstadt Laws, which precluded a city-initiated betrayal, but they in no way prevented Albany from reneging on its own commitment to phase out rent regulations. The protection afforded owners and lenders in 1971 was like an umbrella taken away at the first sight of rain.

The Section 421(a) Betrayal

By 1982, both city and state governments showed signs of wavering on their commitment to deregulate properties falling under the provisions of Section 421 after they were paying full taxes. The first Section 421-subsidized properties that were built after ETPA had been passed were now eight years old. At that time, the rent-stabilization code required owners to offer tenants renewal leases with their choice of one-, two-, or three-year terms. Some owners offered only one- and two-year leases, reasoning that they were not obliged to

grant three-year leases because that would subject them to stabilization in the buildings' eleventh year, by which time full taxes would
be paid.

City Hall and Albany forsook the spirit for the letter of the law and
challenged this interpretation. City officials reasoned that since an
owner was subject to all provisions of the rent-stabilization code, he
would have to follow the code and offer a three-year lease. But the
mere provision of such a lease would subject owners to rent stabilization beyond the date on which benefits ended. Owners were
caught in a legal catch-22.

The next year, the state enacted the Omnibus Housing Act of
1983, which transferred administration of the city's rent regulations
back to the state after twenty-one years of city management. But
Albany proved no more eager to live up to the previous agreement
to deregulate than the city had been. One provision of the Omnibus
Housing Act was to "clarify" the responsibilities of owners of 421(a)
properties; this "compromise" extended rent-stabilization benefits to
existing tenants indefinitely. The fig leaf in front of this breach of
faith was that existing tenants were not adequately informed when
they signed their lease that their apartments were *not* perpetually
rent stabilized. It didn't matter that the rent-stabilization system
could be repealed at any time by the legislature, or that the leases
that had been offered to tenants received prior approval of the state
Division of Housing and Community Renewal (DHCR). Nor did it
matter that DHCR had never even suggested that such wording
should be included.

Pre-1984 tenants received rent-stabilization benefits permanently
with the promised decontrol occurring upon vacancy. Post-1984
tenants received rent-stabilization benefits only for the ten-year period of the building's tax abatement, provided that their initial and
all future leases clearly stated in 24 point type (one-quarter-of-an-
inch tall) that the apartment was to be deregulated after the specified
ten years. If history is any guide, once a sizable number of units go
to the free market, there will be pressure to betray even this betrayal.

The Attempted Betrayal of Mitchell-Lama

In the early 1950s, the state's Joint Legislative Committee on Housing and Multiple Dwellings was alarmed at the lack of construction

of middle income housing. After years of deliberation, the committee advocated stimulating the construction of middle income housing by providing low interest, tax exempt financing, and by permitting partial municipal real estate tax exemption to builders. To receive these benefits, the participating developer agreed to limit his profits and dividends to a fixed return of 6 percent on investment for an extended period of time, thus keeping rent levels at a minimum.

In 1955, the legislature enacted the Limited-Profit Housing Companies Law, more commonly known as the Mitchell-Lama law in recognition of the efforts of Senator MacNeil Mitchell and Assemblyman Al Lama, its principal sponsors. But, initially, there were no takers. Senator Mitchell recalled:

> After two or three years . . . it became apparent to me and to other members of the Joint Legislative Committee that very few housing developers were being attracted to participate in the new program. While the low interest loans and the municipal tax exemption enabled the developments to be built and rented at low costs, the limited 6 percent annual return and lack of potential capital appreciation were serious disincentives to private sector involvement; some other incentive appeared to be necessary to stimulate private investment. [The committee] determined that the prohibition of voluntary dissolution for 35 years, and then only with the consent of the housing commissioner, was the primary disincentive to private sector involvement (*Winthrop Gardens, et al. v. Eimicke*, 1977).

In 1959, the legislature remedied this flaw by reducing the minimum dissolution period to fifteen years and eliminating the need for the housing commissioner's approval for a dissolution. A year later, the legislature again amended the law, increasing the dissolution period to twenty years, while retaining the provision that the housing commissioner's consent would not be required. Virtually all of the Mitchell-Lama housing developments were built under this latter agreement. As Senator Mitchell observed: "This 20-year voluntary dissolution provision, in its entirety, became a permanent essential element of the successful statutory scheme to encourage private free enterprise to invest in these regulated companies and soon resulted in a flood of applications from prospective sponsors and an immediate spurt of building activity throughout the state" (ibid).

In July 1988, two Mitchell-Lama companies exercised their right to prepay their mortgages, dissolve, and become free from regulation by the state Division of Housing and Community Renewal. But then-state Housing Commissioner William Eimicke refused to accept the owners' payment of the outstanding balance, and promulgated a new set of regulations requiring the submission of a detailed notice of intent to dissolve at least 180 days prior to the anticipated date of dissolution. Eimicke's ruling also required a formal public notice, numerous public hearings, and a certificate of no objection from the commissioner, *despite the fact* that the existing law provided for dissolution "without the consent of the commissioner or the supervising agency." Three months later, three additional housing companies with projects financed by the city also sought to prepay their loans only to be refused by the city housing commissioner.

Yet the impact of this ongoing betrayal is completely lost on New York's elected officials. In 1985, Mayor Koch urged private builders to help ease the shortage of housing the city's major builders by constructing affordable housing. The mayor's request amounted to a public challenge made in the form of an open letter with a list of recipients given out to the press. In Mayor Koch's appeal, Mitchell-Lama housing was singled out for praise as an existing program that produced large amounts of privately built affordable housing. Yet at the same time that they were requesting more help, both City Hall and Albany were rewarding those who had built the affordable housing in the past by making them wish they hadn't.

Alas, the concept that past commitments *should* be honored has apparently never taken root in Albany. In the world of New York politics, a deal is never a deal, but a new basis from which to bargain.

7

Zoning New York

One more reason the shortage of rental housing caused by rent control hasn't been satiated by new construction is that, since 1961, New York City has imposed rigid land-use controls. Overlapping layers of land-use regulation—a new zoning code, repeated zoning amendments, environmental reviews, community hearings, and historic landmark designations—have discouraged new construction, further aggravating the city's shortage of rental housing.

Origins of the 1916 Ordinance

In the nineteenth century, zoning laws in New York and most U.S. cities were minimal or nonexistent. By 1901, however, the crowded conditions of immigrant workers, and their willingness to live in tall apartment buildings with very little light and ventilation, led to requirements such as thirty-foot backyards that would bring light and air into the apartment rooms. By 1916, pressure from property owners—who worried that the construction of new skycsrapers and manufacturing sites in residential neighborhoods might hurt the values of adjacent properties—led to New York City's passage of the nation's first zoning ordinance. The ordinance placed limitations on the height and use of new buildings and regulated the juxtaposition of "incompatible" land uses.

The height limitation created five different types of districts, wherein the height of the building at the sidewalk would be determined by the width of the street in front of the property. In a "two-times" district, for example, a new building could be built flush to the property line to a height that was twice the width of the street. An imaginary diagonal line, known as the "sky exposure" plane, would then be drawn from the middle of the street to this two-times point, extending inward and upward toward the sky. The building might then rise above the height of the two-times point, provided that it did not pierce the plane. The invention of the sky-exposure plane created the familiar architectural style of "setbacks" or staircase-like notches atop buildings built in the 1916–61 era that can still be seen today along most of Manhattan's major avenues.

The use restrictions established a spatial segregation of developments that might otherwise impose "external costs" on neighboring properties. Under this criterion, three types of districts were created: residential, commercial, and unrestricted (also known as manufacturing). Residences were deemed to create no external costs and could be located anywhere in the city; offices could locate in a commercial or manufacturing zone; and warehouses and factories could be located only in manufacturing districts.

The city justified these use and height restrictions by citing growing concerns over traffic congestion, ventilation, health, and safety. Amenity requirements such as windows for tenement housing were also justified on these grounds. These provisions for health and safety allowed the city and state to claim "police power" as the constitutional basis for limiting the rights of property owners.

The 1916 zoning ordinance proved to be a model for modern zoning laws in the United States. The New York-type of zoning came to be known as "wedding cake" zoning because the building height and setback requirements encouraged the development of wide buildings that became thinner as they rose from their base.

The most important aspect of the 1916 code, however, was the priority given to housing. The exclusion of industrial and commercial businesses from large areas of upper Manhattan, Brooklyn, and the Bronx clearly enhanced the quality of the residential districts that would be developed in the early twentieth century. And not only was the tradition established of protecting residential areas from commercial encroachment, but apartment buildings and single-family homes could be constructed in any part of the city. Over the forty-five years that the 1916 code was in place, amendments watered down some aspects of the wedding cake structure, but the spirit of the code held that housing development needed no justification and would not drive down the value of surrounding property. Indeed, the first years of the code's implementation saw massive housing construction, with over 80,000 housing units going up per year between 1925 and 1929; by comparison, the construction rate has averaged less than 10,000 units since 1976 (New York City Department of City Planning, 1984).

The 1961 Zoning Ordinance

In 1953, Robert Wagner was elected Mayor with an agenda that included a desire to "re-make the city" through comprehensive government planning. Wagner shared many of the values of the liberal Reform movement, including a concern that skyscraper development in "high districts" of midtown Manhattan would impinge on residential neighborhoods. Just as important as the demands of Reform politicians, however, was a change in architectural fashion.

Influenced by the Seagram Building in Manhattan, which provided an open plaza on Park Avenue, architects criticized the monotony of Manhattan's wedding cake, high-rise construction, favoring instead the replication of the Seagram design, a version of the "Towers in the Park" concept pioneered by the French architect Le Corbusier (Barnett, 1982). According to the Towers philosophy, tall buildings should be set away from the street behind landscaped public plazas. Though the Corbusier concept was implemented, not without serious criticism, in the design of public housing projects (discussed further in Chapter 8), most private developers continued to build to the lot line, filling the envelope permitted by the zoning code. Architects and arbiters of taste wanted to force esthetic changes, and they got their way on December 15, 1960, when the Board of Estimate voted unanimously for what became known as the 1961 Zoning Code (Barnett, 1982).

The 1961 code not only encouraged developers to clone the Seagram building, but created a system of protective or "exclusive" zoning, in which each parcel was restricted to one and only one use. The code created three broad categories of land use: "R zones," "C zones," and "M zones," for residential, commercial, and manufacturing uses respectively. Within each category were finer gradations: residential districts range from R1 to R10, commercial from C1 to

C8, and manufacturing from M1 to M3, with each step indicating a more intensive land use. The intensity of permissible land use within each zone was a function of legal use groups for that zone, and a new density restriction known as the floor-area ratio or FAR. The various possible combinations of use groups and floor-area ratios allowed for a theoretically infinite number of zones.

As the 1961 zoning plan was implemented, however, it became apparent that the city was overzoned for manufacturing. Arbitrary curbs had been placed on residential development in the city's manufacturing areas—Soho, Chelsea, and Clinton in Manhattan, Red Hook in Brooklyn, and Long Island City in Queens. As the economy of the city (and the country) shifted from manufacturing to services, many owners of industrial properties in these areas found that they could not rent out their warehouse and factory space at all, or if they could, they had to do so at rents greatly below those prevalent for commercial or residential space in nearby property.

Overall, manufacturing employment in the city declined by 58 percent between 1950 and 1983. The garment industry, for example, lost 65 percent of its jobs between just 1960 and 1983, and the shoe and toy industries lost 80 percent of their jobs over the same period (Bureau of Labor Statistics, 1984). The space that owners of manufacturing property were left with—tall buildings served by elevators—did not fit the needs of the manufacturing industries that *were* growing in the period. Modern production processes often required long, horizontal factories that could be more easily constructed in New York's suburbs or in other parts of the country. While the city's zoning laws could not have prevented these economic shifts from occurring, the attempt to plan real estate use damaged the city's ability to adapt to changing economic patterns.

The Loft Law

Compelled by the lack of industrial demand in the 1960s and 1970s, many property owners in the manufacturing districts rented out their available space to illegal residential dwellers. The city soon realized that hundreds of loft dwellers were living in apartments that did not meet housing-code standards and were not protected by enforceable leases or by rent controls.

After considerable debate, the city decided in 1976 to legalize the converted lofts. Owners were required to bring the apartments up to code, including putting in walls surrounding makeshift kitchens, and would have to offer leases to their customers. Subsequent rent increases could take into account owners' conversion costs, but would ultimately be governed by the city's new Loft Board.

But rather than open up the manufacturing areas of the city to residential development, the Loft Law actually tightened the land-use controls by creating another bureaucracy and by restricting occupancy in most loft apartments to "artists-in-residence." Under this provision, the old factory buildings of lower Manhattan were designated as artist-only colonies. The law required thousands of sculptors, painters, and designers to submit artwork and prove their artistic credentials in order to obtain an artist's license from the city's Department of Cultural Affairs. As a reward, they became eligible for enormous high-ceilinged living and working space at extremely low rent. Leaving aside the law's Rube Goldberg-like complexity and the absurdity of city bureaucrats determining what is art, the loft laws were yet another attempt by the city to offer rent protection to one favored group while denying opportunities for everyone else. In this case, however, the designation of the favored group took on the character of a medieval craft guild.

Let a Thousand Exceptions Bloom

The special rules incorporated in the loft law are just one example of the unraveling of the premises of the 1961 ordinance. The rigidity and restrictiveness of the zoning framework has created countless unforeseen problems for developers and neighborhoods alike. Developers have not been able to build in many locations under the combination of tight land use and envelope and density constraints. Local residents have often objected even to the structures that could be legally erected in their areas. And certain familiar and treasured facilities and activities have been swept away in the course of development. The response of New York City's planners to these concerns has been to usher in, after 1970, an era of organized and ad hoc zoning exceptions.

One popular rubric for making zoning exceptions has been the naming of a "special district," a sub-zone in the larger fabric with unique rules meant to protect or enhance one or another set of local characteristics. Throughout the 1970s and 1980s special districts were created throughout the city: to keep Manhattan theaters from being demolished, to maintain the vitality of specialized retail areas such as Manhattan's Fifth Avenue, to preserve the architectural character of many residential areas, and to protect wetlands and other natural features. The proliferation of spatial designations leaves the city with over forty special districts today.

Another innovation of exceptionalism was the passage of the "housing quality" program, which uses a scoring system to evaluate proposed housing developments with respect to their architectural and site "quality," giving high marks to structures and sites which reflect current fashions in urban design. Developments that score well on these rules are entitled to less restrictive applications of the regular zoning limits on height, setbacks, lot coverage, and floor area.

The Housing Quality Program is only an instance of a larger "value recapture" philosophy guiding New York's planning and regulation. This has its most frequent application in ad hoc deals negotiated between city officials and developers where specific and idiosyncratic community or infrastructure amenities are traded for zoning leniency, most often greater allowable density. The public benefits can range from new subway stations to community recreation facilities to the retention of an architectural feature. In one of the most publicized (and criticized) applications of this principle, the proposed development on the city owned site of the former Coliseum at Columbus Circle in Manhattan, the "value" being recaptured was actually cash: the zoning concessions vastly increased the city's prospective income from the property's sale.

The ULURP Process

Because of the city's reluctance to change the Zoning Resolution to reflect the need for additional housing, any significant development effort today will almost invariably require a change in the obsolete 1961 ordinance. The amended zoning plan has proven to be so restrictive that over one half of all new construction in the city and virtually all of it in Manhattan now requires some kind of exception to the established as-of-right land-use rules and has essentially prohibited the residential redevelopment of large areas of the city. At one point in the 1970s, the *New York Times* considered as newsworthy the construction of a new office tower without the use of a zoning change (Zabarkes, 1980).

To regularize the process of granting zoning exemption and provide for more community input, the city established the Uniform Land Use Review Process (ULURP) in 1975, which created a procedure for approving or denying any requested zoning changes, large city contracts, or sales of city-owned land; local community boards were given a voice in determining how their neighborhood would change. However, while ULURP was promoted initially as a streamlined six-month process, the review procedure has become an eighteen-month to two-year quagmire that requires developers to prepare lengthy documentation and environmental reviews for their proposals to be "certified" as complete before the six-month clock ever begins to run.

ULURP specifies a 215-day procedure through which all certified proposals for zoning changes and dispositions of city-owned land must proceed. Under the 1990 City Charter, the procedure allows sixty days for community board recommendations, thirty days for borough review, sixty days for City Planning Commission deliberations, sixty days for the City Council to decide on the change, and fifteen days for the Mayor to sign off. If the Mayor disapproves the Council action, the proposal goes back to the Council, which can override the Mayor with a two-thirds vote. Once begun, the ULURP procedure takes "only" two-thirds of a year.

Why does ULURP take so long? Before ever entering the process, the applicant must file his plans with the City Planning Commission and have them certified as "complete." This certification process, which includes the preparation (and approval) of an environmental review, typically takes one to two years.

Within the first sixty-day period, the community board (or boards) in which the project is to be located holds public hearings, examines the proposed project, and makes a recommendation to the city. Although this recommendation is not binding upon any city agency, as representatives of local public opinion the community boards will hold some sway over City Council members.

Appointed by their respective borough presidents, community board members occasionally serve as lightning rods in the political battles between the mayor's administration and the five boroughs.

But while the City Planning Commission (CPC) and the Council will often approve a project that has been rejected by a community board, the boards are frequently able to get a developer to change the design of his project or force him to construct some community facility in order to speed up the approval process.

Some community boards in Manhattan—such as District 3 (Lower East Side), District 4 (Chelsea-Clinton), and District 7 (Upper West Side)—have proven particularly hostile to new development. These and other hostile districts are involved in a large number of development decisions, either because market pressures have made high-rise development economically feasible there, or because the city holds most of the land in the area (the disposition of which triggers the ULURP process).

The other key player in the ULURP game is the CPC and its Department of City Planning. The commission's approval is required for all zoning changes (though not for most other matters involving ULURP). Since the Planning Department can influence and amend projects in the precertification stage, the CPC does not usually vote down many proposals. As in the case of the community boards, formal votes matter less than the informal changes.

Landmarks Preservation

Following the 1961 zoning code, the attention of reformers was drawn to the issue of preserving the city's historic and architecturally significant structures. Until recently, preservation efforts were limited to federal tax credits for the rehabilitation of sites on the National Register of Historic Places, and the acquisition of sites by government through eminent domain. These two methods of preservation became increasingly more difficult for the government to implement. Preservation by use of tax credits depended upon the owner's willingness to use the credits, and on a lack of more profitable alternative uses for the site; preservation by eminent domain required government compensation to owners. Preservation-by-regulation came to seem an attractive alternative which would require neither direct governmental expenditure nor property owners' consent.

What shocked city politicians into action was the demolition of the grand old Penn Station train terminal in order to construct the new Madison Square Garden and a high-rise office complex. To prevent further demolitions of historic or architecturally significant structures, the city passed the 1965 Landmarks Preservation Act. The act established an eleven-member Landmarks Preservation Commission (LPC) appointed by the mayor to designate individual buildings or historic districts as landmarks. The commission could designate any structure over thirty years old that had "a special character or special historical or esthetic interest or value as part of the development, heritage, or cultural characteristics of the city, state, or nation" (Rose, 1985).

Once any property was designated a landmark, its owner would be prevented from demolishing it or making major alterations without the approval of the LPC. Minor changes such as replacing doors or windows or installing an air conditioner or a business sign would require an LPC permit. New construction on a vacant lot in a landmarked district would need approval from the LPC stipulating that the architectural character of the district would not be harmed. The act did contain a hardship provision, which permitted a demolition or major alterations if the landmarked property failed to make a 6 percent profit on investment for its owner, but this provision would prove more difficult to utilize in practice than in theory. Under this hardship provision, only five landmarked buildings have been demolished to date.

Unlike the City Planning Commission's decisions, the LPC designations would become effective immediately, and would stand unless the Board of Estimate (now City Council) voted to modify or veto its actions. (By contrast, the CPC needed a three-fourths vote of the Board of Estimate to approve its zoning decisions.) The Landmarks Commission would have to meet only minimal criteria in order to claim that a building or district had a historic character, and its decisions would never have to face any community board or city planning review. In effect, the Landmarks Commission became an independent arm of government, without sufficient checks or balances from an elected body of city government or any accountability to the public at large.

The Constitutionality of Landmarking

Given that it denies owners full use of their properties, does the Landmarks Preservation Act violate the constitutional prohibition against the taking of private property for public use without compensation? Unlike the city's zoning powers, landmarking is suspect because of its impact on *individual* sites: rather than broad areas. If the city tightened the zoning resolution for a single building, the Supreme Court would consider that to be a "spot zoning" and, under the Constitution, a "taking that would require compensation to the owner."

The city, concerned that its landmarking rules might be challenged, established a compensation mechanism by granting to owners of landmarked property the right to sell any unused zoning rights on landmarked property. Under the transferable development-rights provision (TDR) the unused square-footage or FAR (floor-area ratio) of a landmark building can be sold and then added to the allowable FAR of an adjacent property, provided the new FAR of the non-landmarked building is increased by no more than 20 percent of the original zoning entitlement. The theory is that the loss in value from landmarking is compensated by sale of the property's development rights. In practice, however, much of the development rights of landmarked property are not transferable, either because potential recipient sites cannot accept any additional FARs, or because the buildings on those sites are in good condition and are not yet ready to be replaced.

The takings question was finally brought to the U.S. Supreme Court in 1978 by the Penn Central Corporation, owners of the Grand Central train station, who were challenging LPC's disapproval of a proposed office tower to sit astride the terminal. The Court ruled 6 to 3 that the Landmarks Commission *was* exercising the city's police powers after the manner of zoning, and that even if a particular landmark designation was a taking, the TDR provision and the hardship provision allowed sufficient compensation to owners. In an equally strong dissent, Justice Rehnquist called landmarking "spot zoning" and the TDR provision totally inadequate as a compensation mechanism. At a very minimum, Rehnquist considered that Penn Central should be compensated some $3 million per year for lost rent receipts because of the action of the LPC *(Penn Central Transportation Company v. City of New York)*. While the matter seemed settled in 1978, the appointment of several new justices (Scalia, O'Connor, Kennedy) with stronger views on property rights and the presence of two of the original dissenters (Rehnquist, Stevens) has made reconsideration of the takings issue a possibility.

Since 1978, the commission has approved about two new historic districts per year, including large sections of central Brooklyn and Manhattan's East and West sides. By 1984, the commission had landmarked some 690 individual buildings, 44 historic districts including some 16,000 buildings, and 45 building interiors (Rose, 1985). The most recent landmarking activities include some fairly rarefied concepts. The LPC has landmarked a "historic scenic view"—the view of Manhattan from Brooklyn Heights, which under the Manhattan Scenic View Historic District may not be interrupted by any high-rise construction on the waterfront below the Heights. And the LPC has invented the landmarking of neon lighting such as the various Times Square advertising displays and the Pepsi-Cola sign on the East River waterfront in Queens.

In a strange way, the landmarking process has become a response to, and a substitute for, the damage that the new zoning code has done to the city's architecture. The FAR bonuses for plaza construction, low income housing, transit improvements, and the like have allowed developers to pierce the "zoning envelope," the traditional, pre-1961 ceiling on building heights. The maximum lot coverage provision of the code, which sought to promote open space and plazas, has also directly changed the architectural character of several neighborhoods by ending the straight lines of the avenues and the wedding cake apartment buildings and encouraging the development of unusually tall and thin towers out of character with their neighbors. The magnificent vistas of Park Avenue or Fifth Avenue that, in a sense, were created by the 1916 zoning code, are threatened by the present code. Rather than return to the old zoning format, however, the neighborhood preservationists have asked for special zoning districts or sought landmark status to "freeze" the neighborhood character and style. And since any special neighborhood-rezoning proposal requires their navigating the time-consuming ULURP process, the more expedient recourse is to assert some architectural or historic significance and seek landmark designation. Landmarking and simple zoning may achieve the same end result, but involve very different costs.

Finally, the transfer of development rights to adjacent buildings has had unforeseen yet significant consequences. The South Street Seaport Historic District in Lower Manhattan is now surrounded by skyscrapers built using transferable development rights obtained from buildings in the district. Buildings located in the middle of the district, however, are unable to sell their development rights because all neighboring buildings are protected, and they often stand in disrepair because they are unable to acquire the funds that are needed for restoration. Therefore, rather than retaining the character of an eighteenth-century fishing village—the official rationalization for landmark status—the Seaport has become a low-rise valley among the skyscrapers of the insurance and banking industry and a happy-hour entertainment district for downtown office workers.

The full expression of the power of the Landmarks Commission came with the designation of the Upper East Side Historic District in 1981. Most of the architecturally important churches, town houses, and brownstones on East Side were already individually designated, yet in a sweeping move the commission landmarked some sixty city blocks containing 1,044 individual buildings, blocking several proposed apartment towers in the process (Rose, 1985). Unlike the earlier precedent of Brooklyn Heights and the Soho/Cast Iron Historic Districts, the Upper East Side District does not form any homogeneous area of a unique building style. Indeed, in its designation report, the Landmarks Commission noted the *eclectic* character of buildings in the area, citing some forty-five different architectural styles in all.

In creating the new district, the city closed off perhaps the most desirable residential area in the city to new development, and for this reason creation of the district was strongly criticized by architects, respected preservationists, dissenting commission members, and critics in the media. While drawing a direct connection between historic landmarking and housing construction may be difficult, we note that the rate of new housing construction in the community district containing the historic district fell dramatically after 1981, even though construction city-wide remained more or less constant. Between 1977 and 1981, the construction rate was 1,136 apartment units per year in the area and 8,952 per year city-wide. Between 1982 and 1985, the area rate fell to 206 while the city-wide rate was 8,500 per year (New York City Department of City Planning, 1986). The unstated and (possibly) unintended effect of the Upper East Side District designation has been to say, in effect, *this area already houses enough people.* The burden of new housing must either be taken by other neighborhoods or must lead to a rise in the city's cost of housing.

In some cases, the landmarking process has actually led to the destruction of existing properties. Without compensation, owners will always prefer that their building *not* become landmarked; in several cases, they have even attempted to demolish or disfigure their buildings to prevent designation. The commission's response to this phenomenon has been to accelerate the designation process by getting the Buildings Department to refuse to issue demolition or alteration permits within even *proposed* landmark districts.

Beyond its possible legal liability to compensate property owners, the city bears a fiscal burden from landmarking. Courts have consistently lowered property tax assessments following landmark designations, leading to a loss of property tax revenue. The loss of developable land or increased costs from LPC permit acquisition is reflected in higher housing costs. Finally, the creation of transferable development rights means that designating historic districts will lead to increased development above the zoning envelope on surrounding properties, distorting the overall character of the city and reducing the efficiency of housing production.

Conclusion

The expansion of land-use controls in the last thirty years has made it harder for new housing development to end New York City's housing shortage, and to compensate for the effects of rent regulation. Why has development regulation become so restrictive? New York's rapid economic and demographic changes have produced a backlash against any kind of corresponding physical change or growth, as certain threatened sectors and groups work to freeze development to protect their positions. For example, unions and manufacturers have managed to cordon off the city's waterfront areas from new residential and commercial development, a holding action that will only intensify redevelopment pressure. Homeowners have fought fiercely to keep their neighborhoods free of dreaded apartment buildings, only making it that much more difficult for their friends and children to obtain an apartment. Artists have won their protected place in the city, only to find that grimy industrial districts like Soho and Chelsea have become trendy hangouts for fashion artists and graphics designers.

In the long run, of course, these development restrictions may be futile. As long as New York remains an exciting and profitable place to live, and as long as New Yorkers find innovative ways to get past or around land-use regulations, housing production will never quite reach zero. Yet, until the day when the city removes its stringent barriers to building, the cost of this new housing will remain unconscionably high.

8

The Hidden Tax on Housing

Although rent and land-use controls have been the most controversial forms of housing regulation in New York City, a less controversial but perhaps more damaging restriction on the housing supply has been the real estate property tax. The current system of property taxation has discouraged construction and encouraged abandonment; it has reduced the supply of available housing and raised unregulated rents. High property tax rates have also forced the city to pursue a wasteful policy of tax abatement, and in all probability have stunted the city's economic growth. With prospects for reform hindered by a lack of citizen concern and by the electoral influence of current beneficiaries, any viable reform package must address the concerns of both the apathetic and the vested.

Assessment Inequality

Under New York City's nearly unique property tax system, owners of apartment buildings bear an unusually high proportion of the tax burden. Because Albany legislators have long feared that taxing all property equally might generate a homeowners' revolt or create the need for massive spending cuts, this skewed situation has existed for decades. It was most recently codified in a 1981 state law, by which city real estate is divided into four categories; each category is assessed and taxed at a different rate. As can be seen, the assessment rates for Classes II, III, and IV are four to five times the rate on Class I, which includes all one-, two-, and three-family homes. In other

Table 8.1. 1986 Tax and assessment rates (percentages)

	Class	(1) Nominal tax rate	(2) Assessment rate	(1) × (2) Effective tax rate
I	Homeowner	9.33	11.69	1.09
II	Other residential	9.15	48.83	4.47
III	Utility	9.172	56.07	5.14
IV	Commerical	9.46	53.97	5.11

Source: New York State Board of Equalization and Assessement.

words, homeowners get off lightly, while owners of apartment build-ings and commercial structures bear a property tax burden out of all proportion to their share of market value. Also, because a provision of the 1981 state law requires that each property class contribute to property tax collections in proportion to its "historic share," the city has very little leeway to adjust the system's inequalities. Even if the city chose to assess all property at the same rate tomorrow, it would have to set low nominal tax rates for homeowners, and very high rates for commercial, utility, and rental properties, in order to collect revenues of "historic" proportions.

As a result of this tax policy, the 33 percent of New Yorkers who are homeowners pay one of the lowest tax rates in the country, while owners of apartment buildings, who house two-thirds of all New York households, pay one of the highest. In a recent survey of property tax rates in twenty-two of the nation's largest cities, New York had the highest rate on apartment buildings.

Assessing for Abandonment

In theory, taxes should never be so high as to make any property completely unprofitable. As the value of the property falls, so should the assessment. Unfortunately, city tax administrators are reluctant to adjust assessments downward. Some errors may be eventually corrected, but the city's high effective rate of property taxation makes these errors very costly to property owners. Failure by the city to quickly adjust its assessment of a rental property to reflect reduc-tions in its rental income may wipe out the building's profits. Since

Table 8.2. Effective property tax rates in major U.S. cities, 1986–87 (percentages)[a]

City	Homeowner	Rental	Commercial
	East		
New York	1.12	4.13	4.66
Philadelphia	2.39	2.39	2.39
Boston	1.06	1.20	2.36
Washington	0.98	1.44	1.79
Baltimore	2.31	2.70	2.70
Pittsburgh	2.96	3.05	3.15
	Midwest		
Chicago	1.91	2.83	4.04
Detroit	3.52	4.08	4.08
Cleveland	1.83	1.83	2.07
Minneapolis	1.18	3.58	4.95
St. Louis	0.96	3.24	3.24
	South		
Dallas	0.92	1.28	1.28
Houston	1.01	1.46	1.46
Atlanta	2.00	2.00	2.00
Miami	1.66	2.45	2.45
Tampa	1.26	1.89	1.89
San Antonio	1.05	1.26	1.26
	West		
Los Angeles	0.72	0.52	0.72
San Francisco	0.71	0.74	0.74
San Diego	0.62	0.65	0.65
Phoenix	1.10	1.86	2.74
Seattle	1.29	1.29	1.29

Source: Interviews with state and local tax-assessment authorities.

a. The effective rate is a multiplication of the nominal tax rate times the assessment rate. Allowances were made for universal homestead exemptions or tax credits, but not for targeted exemptions (for the elderly or the poor, for example) or targeted abatements (for new construction or rehabiliatation).

post-tax profits determine the value of the building to its owner, systematic overassessment can drive a building's value to zero.

For precisely this reason, tens of thousands of New York City owners with enormous property tax liabilities have abandoned their buildings in recent years (Salins, 1980). It has been reliably estimated that over 30,000 city apartment units were abandoned between 1968 and 1978 alone (Lowry, 1985). This syndrome of tax-driven abandonment has been especially common in the poorest areas of the city, where property values have plunged but tax assessments have remained fairly constant.[1] Because the city's tax policy mandates the rapid acquisition of abandoned buildings, and its housing policy favors keeping rather than selling them, the city currently owns some 10,000 of these abandoned "in rem" properties, virtually all of them in poor areas like Harlem and the South Bronx. Of these, 5,700 are completely vacant, while maintenance of the remainder costs the city over $200 million each year.

Though some units are, of course, abandoned for reasons unrelated to property assessment, a recent study by Michelle J. White found the level of property taxation to be a more significant contributor to delinquency rates than several other possible causes: the age of buildings, the income of neighborhood residents, the percentage of residents on welfare, the percentage of single-family homes, and the percentage of tenement structures. Estimating, moreover, that a 1 percent rise in property taxes was associated with a 2.1 percent rise in tax delinquency rates, White reasoned that under the existing city policy of taking over and subsidizing tax-delinquent "in rem" housing properties, the city actually *loses* money by keeping property taxes so high in the city's poorest neighborhoods.

Although White acknowledged that cutting property taxes $1,000 per building (6 percent) in a typical poor neighborhood—Brownsville, Brooklyn—would cost the city $109,000 per year, her regression results suggested there would be 60 fewer tax delinquent properties in the neighborhood—yielding some $86,000 per year in recovered tax revenue. Furthermore, assuming that one-quarter of these 60 buildings would otherwise have to be managed in the city's "in rem" program in the event of tax delinquency, a lower tax rate would save the city another $208,000. Therefore, the impact of property taxation rates on abandonment would create something like a local Laffer Curve, whereby the city could gain more from having a larger property tax base, and smaller "in rem" subsidies, than it would lose from a lower property tax rate in poor neighborhoods (White, 1986).

Property Tax Rates and Competitiveness

While White's neighborhood-based, hypothetical case suggests that lower property taxes may mean more housing in the city and more money in its treasury, actual larger-scale examples indicate that property tax cuts may jumpstart a region's economy. The beneficial economic effects of lower property tax rates appear to be validated by recent property tax revolts in California and Massachusetts, which were followed by high rates of economic growth. Although economists have hotly debated whether these state-wide property tax cuts actually caused economic expansion, the possible linkage of taxation and economic growth seems especially relevant to high-tax states like New York.

In Massachusetts, where the property tax rate previously *averaged* 4.4 percent, the passage of Proposition 2 1/2 in 1980 set a 2.5 percent *maximum* rate cap for any individual piece of property. Four years later, state-wide property tax collections were still 6.5 percent below their 1981 peak, but property values and employment rose dramatically (Brookes, 1986).

A similarly suggestive model is California's Proposition 13, which cut property tax rates from 2.47 percent to 1.20 percent with strict ceilings on assessment increases. Under Proposition 13, assessments on any individual piece of property are permitted to rise by no more than 2 percent annually unless the property is sold (at which time, the sale price becomes the assessment). With nominal rates capped and assessments lagging further behind market values (due to real estate inflation above 2 percent and low turnover of property), California's effective tax rates have continued to fall. Property tax receipts have only now returned to their 1977–78 peak.

Although both states have seen their economies sour in the 1990–1992 recession, in both Massachusetts and California property tax cuts appear to have produced a substantial economic payoff when they were first implemented. From 1975 to 1984 the number of jobs increased by 25.5 percent in Massachusetts and by 34.5 percent in

California, compared to gains of 21.5 percent in the rest of the country and a meager 10.6 percent in high-tax New York State.

If the cases of California and Massachusetts are any indication, a large cut in New York City's property tax, especially if concentrated on its rental property, would not only have important beneficial impacts on the housing supply but could also put the city in a better position to compete for its share of the nation's business.

The Tax Abatement Solution: Part of the Problem?

Although economists have yet to agree on the exact nature of the relation between tax cuts and economic growth, New York City already acts as if lower taxes promote the retention of more taxable enterprise. In fact, it offers tax breaks to special segments of the population on just these grounds. But it provides these tax breaks to help house the rich and powerful instead of the middle class and the poor.

Because its high tax rates on commercial and rental properties encourage individuals and business to relocate in neighboring towns or competing regions, New York City has relied on special tax reductions, or abatements, in order to retain business and encourage the construction of new rental housing. Some tax abatements are granted automatically, as in the case of new apartment buildings or rental-unit rehabilitation. Others are granted as part of "job retention" or "job creation" packages when businesses threaten to relocate. These abatements have been criticized as favoring only the sectors with access to city officials, and subjecting the city to fiscal blackmail.

Yet given the city's high revenue needs and the state-mandated policy of assessment, abatements are virtually unavoidable. If a developer had to pay a 5 percent property tax on his just completed apartment building instead of phasing in full taxes over several years, the higher rents needed to earn a competitive return would prevent any new apartment construction at all.

But is the city giving away too much? Is a five-year phase-in period sufficient to promote new construction, or would a ten-year period be more effective? If a business threatens to leave the city unless its taxes are reduced, how does the city determine if the threat is credible? Is the size of the tax break too low, too high, or just right? Who's to know?

The city's ad hoc policy of tax abatements comes down to a policy of greasing only the squeaky wheels and cutting taxes only for those businesses deemed most "in need," which usually turn out to be large or well connected firms. Instead of continuing this unequitable and inefficient policy, the city could eliminate the tax breaks, *reduce* its rental property tax rates by 13 percent, and *still* collect the same amount of revenue.[2]

Obstacles to Reform

With tax abatement helping all the wrong people, and with high property taxes causing abandonment and probably stunting economic growth, why doesn't the city lower its property tax rates?

Since it is clear that state legislators are unlikely to equalize property assessments, landlords have often wondered whether there might be a constitutional way to limit their property tax burden. These owners are usually surprised to hear that New York already *does* have a constitutional limit on property tax: the state constitution places a limit on New York City's property levy at 2.5 percent of the full value of its property tax base.

Several provisions in the constitution and the administration of the tax system, however, make this limitation completely ineffective. Perhaps most significantly, the constitution exempts from its limitation the revenue needed to pay the city's long-term debt. Thus, ongoing deficits in the sixties and seventies have permitted the city to levy property taxes today far in excess of the 2.5 percent limit.[3]

The real problem, however, lies not in the the state constitution but in city voters' perception that property tax rates do not matter very much. Why should the average renter care what the property tax is? Would lowering the tax rate ever lower his monthly outlay? Hardly ever, if the tenant pays a below-market rent. The only time when the property tax *directly* affects the tenant is at the rare but cataclysmic point of abandonment. Once a landlord has accumulated years of unpaid tax bills, however, tinkering with that tax rate will do little for the owner or the tenant.

By contrast, a homeowner's interest in the property tax is very direct—but, alas, only concerning his individual assessment. If he owns a single-family (Class I) unit, he is the beneficiary of a property tax system designed to keep him from fleeing to the suburbs. The homeowner has little reason to complain about high property taxes on multi-family units. In fact, he is likely to oppose any adjustment of tax policy and property assessments favoring rental properties that might cause him to bear more of the tax burden.

Because of renter indifference, and because single-family homeowners currently benefit from assessment inequality, New York City's property tax policy is seldom debated at all. When the mayor presents his budget every spring, the property tax rate is a *fait accompli*. Single-family homeowners sometimes complain about increased assessments and tax bills, but their deal is already so good, relative to other property owners, that legislators cannot help them without reducing overall property tax revenues. The only controversial property tax issue is the granting of large tax abatements to luxury developers and businesses. Reformers urge the repeal of these tax breaks so that the money can be spent on other programs and projects; the city maintains that the tax breaks are needed to broaden its employment base and to encourage construction.

So, although a reduced property tax rate would benefit renters, run-down neighborhoods, and the city's economy generally, the institutional and political setting make reform difficult to implement.

Prospects for Reform

The benefits from current tax policy are concentrated among relatively well-to-do homeowners in the outer boroughs, but benefits from reduced property-tax rates would be widely dispersed. In any case, the support, or at least the acquiescence, of New York City homeowners would be needed to adjust the current system. Property tax reform thus needs to be proposed and considered as a political package that would guarantee the position of current beneficiaries.

To begin with, any viable reform package might have to leave intact the present low tax rates on one-, two-, and three-family homes. The 1.12 percent effective tax rate for homeowners is quite low, but not any lower than the rates in Boston, Washington, D.C., and all the major cities of California and Texas.

Another necessary component of any package would be a more

effective constitutional tax limitation. The city's power to raise its tax limitation by issuing more debt should be curtailed while at the same time the effective cap should be implemented at the level of the individual property owner. The power to enforce the tax limitation should not rest with local government officials or the state controller, but with property owners, who would be empowered to challenge their own effective tax rates.[4]

Perhaps the best model for making a tax limitation an individual right is the Massachusetts' Proposition 2 1/2, which capped the nominal property tax rate for any individual property at 2.5 percent. Since previous tax rates were much higher, this ceiling dramatically reduced most tax bills. Local officials then sought to increase assessments to full market value to maximize revenue, making assessments easier for the public to understand, to evaluate, and to challenge if inaccurate.

That kind of reform is exactly the package that New York needs. Tax rates on homeowners might be kept at or near their current moderate levels. But rates should be reduced dramatically for apartment owners and commercial property owners. The key to adopting such a reform, however, is to convince a city of renters that reduced property tax rates would help them; that it would discourage abandonment and encourage construction, increasing the supply of available housing and lowering unregulated rents.

9

Public Housing by Default

New York's inferior housing conditions, the legacy of rent regulation and other housing market distortions, has persuaded low income tenants and their advocates that the only effective option for improving their housing is to become tenants of the government. The most persistent political response to New York's housing crisis has thus been the promotion of the construction of publicly financed, often publicly developed, sometimes publicly owned and managed housing. In many of the city's low income neighborhoods half of the housing units and most of the developable land is owned by New York City. But this dependence on public housing creates as many distortions in the low income housing market as rent regulation imposes on the city's middle income housing supply. Reliance on public housing has reduced the city's tax base, increased direct subsidies from the treasury, adversely affected surrounding neighborhoods, prevented the construction of new housing, caused more than 130,000 currently vacant apartment units to be unavailable for rent, and created a political environment where the effects of rent regulation on the poor remain hidden from public debate.

A Tradition of Public Housing Leadership

New York City today boasts of having the largest public housing sector of any city in the country. Not only was the concept of public housing in the United States initiated here, but several recent innovations in New York have expanded the public sector's involvement

Table 9.1. Direct public housing expenditures in New York City, 1986

Program	Expenditures (thousands of dollars)	Source of funds		
		Federal	State	Local
AFDC shelter allowances	563,328	50.0	25.0	25.0
Other shelter allowances	285,058	0.0	50.0	50.0
Public housing	332,285	89.6	4.0	6.5
Section 8/vouchers	28,965	100.0	0.0	0.0
Homeless housing	231,035	28.8	35.8	35.4
In rem housing	176,555	48.8	0.0	51.2
Code enforcement	37,733	22.3	13.3	64.4
Rehabilitation programs	48,433	100.0	0.0	0.0
Other programs	71,053	8.4	69.0	22.6
Total	1,774,445	46.4	24.4	29.2

Source: Citizens Budget Commission, 1987.

to include the rehabilitation of abandoned apartment buildings at city expense, the construction of enormous high-rise mini-cities, and the subsidization of the management of numerous public projects by tenant committees. The total amount spent on housing, $1.77 billion, is nearly 9 percent of the entire city budget for 1986—$20 billion.

An important part of public policy absent from the table of direct expenditures is tax expenditures. Tax expenditures are those tax dollars that are not collected because of exemptions or abatements in the income tax or the property tax codes. The greatest beneficiaries of local property tax policy are the public housing projects and the Mitchell-Lama program.

Approximately 500,000 residents live in the 166,000 apartment units managed by the New York City Housing Authority, a federally subsidized local agency which owns 6.2 percent of the city's housing units—almost three times the national average. Looked at in another way, New York City, with 3.2 percent of the nation's population, has 7.7 percent of the nation's supply of federally subsidized housing units.

The original intent of public housing was to improve the physical environment of the city's low income neighborhoods. Reformers in the early twentieth century, concerned that the crowded and unsan-

Table 9.2. Local tax expenditures for housing in New York City, 1986
(in thousands of dollars)

Program	Estimated forgone revenue
N.Y.C. Housing Authority	$ 194,600
Other (mostly Mitchell-Lama)	187,800
J-51 exemptions	75,200
J-51 abatements	61,000
421-a	73,000
421-b	9,900
Senior citizens exemptions	9,000
Senior citizens rent increase exemptions	45,000
Veterans exemptions	9,800
Total	$ 665,300
Total property tax revenue	$4,868,000

Sources: Citizens Budget Commission, 1987; New York City Comptroller, 1986.

itary conditions of tenement housing were inhumane, promoted new building codes requiring developers to install indoor plumbing facilities and provide a minimum amount of light and air for each apartment. The reformers also advocated public construction of new apartments to relocate the city's poor from cramped and dilapidated tenements.

Toward this end, the city tore down many of the existing tenements and in 1929 revised its building codes. Subsequent new construction would have to include separate bathrooms in each apartment and windows for each room. If you see a New York City apartment today with a bathroom down the hall or one with a windowless room, you know the apartment was built before 1929 and was grandfathered under the building code.

In 1926 Governor Al Smith prompted the state legislature to approve his Limited Dividend Housing Program, the first peacetime government housing program in the nation. The public housing concept was eventually brought to Washington as part of Roosevelt's New Deal; in the U.S. Housing Act of 1937, Congress imitated the efforts in New York and passed the first federally assisted public housing program.

In the early public housing "projects," prescribed rent levels were the same for all apartments of the same size and were set sufficiently high to cover the building's operating costs. The chief subsidy in the program was the underwriting of initial construction costs by the federal government. Construction costs were financed by floating low-interest federal, state, or city bonds whose debt service was paid by the federal government. In addition, local governments exempted housing projects from property tax.

Local housing authorities decided who would live in the housing projects. According to guidelines that governed the program until 1969, tenants became eligible if their income was high enough to pay the rent but did not exceed five times (later expanded to six times) the rent. Tenants who were displaced by the demolition of tenement buildings on the project site were supposed to receive priority placements in the new apartment buildings, though this apparent preference was by no means universally or equitably implemented.

Because rents were based on an apartment's share of the building's total costs, the original concept of the public housing program treated all tenants equally and had no inherent welfare component. The program was perceived as workers' housing and not as welfare housing.

After World War II, the federal government greatly expanded public housing by financing large-scale construction throughout the country. In this case, "large scale" meant both an enormous number of new units and apartment buildings ten, fifteen, and twenty stories tall—often in neighborhoods of three-story brownstones.

These new public housing projects revolutionized the appearance of American cities and were very controversial within the development community. A new generation of architects, influenced by Le Corbusier's "Ville Radieuse" plan for Marseilles, sought to change the city's seemingly endless pattern of squat, rectangular apartment buildings, built block after block, all set flush against the property line. They designed new residential towers away from the property lines, often at angles with the street grid to create more interesting vistas and to take maximum advantage of the sunlight. To provide recreation for tenants and their children, parks and playgrounds were built between the buildings, giving many of the projects a campuslike environment.

True to the original goals of the housing reformers, the planners of postwar public housing created an environment for their new tenants very different from the run-down conditions they were used to. The projects were built with unexpected amenities and design features that aimed to vanquish the monotony and dreariness of living in crowded and shabby urban neighborhoods without adequate parks or open space.

This formula for building subsidized public housing prevailed for twenty years after World War II. Local authorities (usually independent from the municipal government) could plan and design new public housing projects and issue bonds for their construction. Federal subsidies would retire the bonds, making the federal financial role that of a onetime capital grant. The residents of the projects were expected to pay rent to the Housing Authority to cover the day-to-day operating costs of the project. Having their rent increases connected to the financial health of the building gave the residents a clear stake in the efficient management of their apartment building. Leaking windows, a broken elevator, or an overpaid employee meant higher rents for the tenants.

This policy broke down in the wake of the inflation of the 1960s. As wages and other operating costs spiraled, rents in public housing rose in step, presenting a growing burden for low income tenants. Congress responded by passing the Housing Act of 1969, popularly known as the Brooke Amendment after Edward Brooke, the liberal Republican senator from Massachusetts, to limit the rent in public housing to one-fourth of the tenant's income.[1] The Brooke Amendment committed Congress to pay the difference between the rent collected and the operating expenses of the authorities.

Under this new policy, the federal government prevented local housing authorities from passing on any of the costs of inflation to the tenants, whether in terms of increased heating bills or electricity charges, janitors' salaries, or management overhead. As a result, an ever-increasing proportion of federal housing funds since 1969 have gone to operating and maintaining the existing supply of public housing—*at the expense of new construction*. Because additional construction of public housing would now have meant massive and perpetual demands on the federal treasury, the switch from capital subsidies to operating subsidies meant that the era of large-scale public housing construction had come to an end.

In any case, officials in the Nixon administration objected to the traditional supply-oriented public housing programs and were eager to see a change in policy. A key criticism was the inefficiency of giving benefits to the poor in the form of housing rather than in cash. Instead of building new public housing projects that might not necessarily reflect the consumption or utility preferences of low income households, they advocated giving the poor "housing vouchers" to assist them in finding an apartment in the private market. This demand-side orientation would allow builders to participate in the federal housing program and would offer more choice to low income recipients, with respect to both cost and quality of their apartments.

Advocates of this approach expected that low income tenants would be able to find more suitable and higher quality apartments in the private market than the government could build. And by offering low income tenants a choice of apartments from throughout the area, the voucher alternative offered the possibility of dispersing the city's low income population rather than concentrating them in a few high-rise projects.

To test this hypothesis, the federal government sponsored a housing demand experiment in the early 1970s in several areas around the country. The perceived success of this experiment emboldened Congress to make housing allowances an important part of the overall federal housing policy, as manifested in the Section 8 program of the Housing Act of 1974.[2] Most federal housing spending since 1974 has gone for public housing rehabilitation or subsidies to individual tenants (rather than to buildings).

More recently, under the Reagan administration, the new generation of federal housing subsidies came under attack. New commitments to the Section 8 program were greatly reduced. Subsidies to the existing public housing projects remained largely intact, if in something of a fiscal limbo. The federal government continued to offer enough money to supplement the tenants' rents and meet the operating costs, but not enough for any dramatic improvements in quality or expansion of the supply.

One possible change in public housing policy may be coming from the other side of the Atlantic. Taking a cue from the Thatcher government's housing-privatization program in Britain, some conservatives in Congress and especially current Housing Secretary Jack Kemp promoted the idea of letting tenants manage the projects themselves or purchase them from local authorities at a minimal cost. These efforts offer some promise.

Replicating the successful British model in the United States would be quite difficult, however. Public housing in Britain is tenanted by the middle class as well as the poor, offering a much larger and more affluent pool of potential home buyers. Moreover, much of the British public housing stock is in single-family houses rather than in high-rise projects, making the home ownership option much more viable. Nevertheless, several projects around the country have already been converted either to tenant management or tenant ownership. The privatization option remains an important alternative for improving New York's housing stock, opening up its housing market, and redirecting federal housing expenditures.

Limited-Profit Housing

To complement traditional public housing, New York State has pioneered several programs of publicly assisted housing that combine small subsidies, private investment, and control. While not suffering from the same levels of crime and physical deterioration as public housing, these projects only augment the distortions of New York's low rent, low vacancy housing market.

The largest of these efforts is the Mitchell-Lama program. The premise of this program, as well as of many subsequent state and federal housing programs, was that middle income tenants were a casualty of government housing policy: too rich to qualify for public housing, but too poor to afford decent private housing. Thus Mitchell-Lama set out to build new developments of self-supporting rental and co-op buildings on the sites of decaying tenement buildings or on large parcels of publicly owned land. Land acquisition, financing, and tax abatement subsidies were to be just large enough to make rents affordable for the middle class, but not so large as to place an "unacceptable" burden on New York taxpayers.

The state program dovetailed with the federal government's urban renewal land-clearance program, which provided subsidies for demolition of slum tenements where new Mitchell-Lama projects could be built. This approach to urban development proved so popular that New York City soon formed its own Mitchell-Lama-type program. From 1955 to 1982, 140,000 apartments were constructed in New York City under the various Mitchell-Lama and limited-profit housing programs, creating an inventory about as large as public housing. Like public housing, Mitchell-Lama developments tended to be quite large and are today concentrated in certain areas of the city. For example, in the community district in the Bronx that includes the massive Co-op City project, 39 percent of the housing units are Mitchell-Lamas. Other areas with high concentrations are:

Queens (Rockaway Peninsula)	35%
Manhattan (Downtown)	33%
Brooklyn (Coney Island-Brighton Beach)	31%
Brooklyn (East New York)	17%
Manhattan (East Harlem)	14%

Mitchell-Lama projects were either rentals or co-ops. In the rental program, the state offered developers long-term, low interest construction loans, cheap vacant land (usually acquired through urban renewal), and substantial property tax abatements. In exchange, the owner agreed to keep rents at a level just high enough to cover operating and maintenance costs and a 6 percent return on investment. Under the original legislation, rents were to be regulated by the 6 percent formula for thirty-five years, after which the developer could appeal to the state housing commissioner to repay his subsidized loans and remove himself from the program. The developer could then charge market rents—provided that he began paying full property taxes.

The combination of a low return and the long commitment period made the program unattractive to developers, and little construction took place in the early years of the Mitchell-Lama program. To make the program more inviting, amendments to the law in 1959 and 1960 removed the discretionary power of the housing commissioner and reduced the control period to twenty years. Construction rates in the combined state and city programs rose from 1,052 units per year in 1958–60 to 4,277 in 1961–63 to 8,990 in 1964–66. Clearly, developers were motivated both by the guaranteed rate of return from a Mitchell-Lama investment and the likely appreciation in value once the program had run its course.

The Mitchell-Lama cooperatives were subsidized on much the same basis as the rentals, but were owned and managed by tenant cooperative boards. However, two quirks in the co-op arrangement made their success unlikely. First, the purchase prices for each co-op share were set very low, and share price appreciation was disallowed. Since they had little equity stake in their building and no possibility of winning capital gains, many cooperators did not consider themselves *real* owners, and viewed their monthly carrying charges as quasi-rental payments.

Another unusual feature of the Mitchell-Lama co-ops was the mortgage. Instead of each individual cooperator having a loan to cover the purchase of his share, the co-op board held a building-wide mortgage, payable to the city or the state. Tenants paid their carrying charges to a management company, which then made payment on the mortgage.

This method of financing dogged the Mitchell-Lama program. As operating costs escalated, tenants often were unwilling to pay higher carrying charges. Since the mortgage was held by a group of tenants rather than by individuals, the state was politically unable to discipline co-op boards that failed to meet their mortgage payments and property tax payments. Angered by shoddy construction and poor services at their projects, several tenant boards actually organized "rent strikes" against themselves, bankrupting their own boards.

The bankruptcies of Mitchell-Lama projects converted the program from being self-financed to one subsidized by the taxpayers. Under these conditions, the expansion of the program could not be continued indefinitely, and additional funding for the program was halted in 1974. The last Mitchell-Lama building was completed in 1980.

"In Rem" Housing

The "in rem" housing sector is less a program than a historical accident that grew out of the city's fiscal crisis of the 1970s. *In rem*, Latin for "against the thing," means a court action against a piece of property for failure to pay taxes, as opposed to *in personam*, an action against a person. Prior to the fiscal crisis, the city had the prerogative of taking title, or "vesting" a property, only after four years of tax delinquency. Traditionally, the city had taken over residential properties as a last resort when property owners failed to pay their taxes; until a vesting or a court order took place, the city had no right to manage or dispose of delinquent property.[3] And even after the vesting, the delinquent owner retained the option for several years of reclaiming his property by paying his overdue liability.

During the fiscal crisis, under pressure to increase property tax collections, city officials decided to reduce the grace period for nonpayment from four years to three, and later from three years to one. They reasoned that delinquent property owners were trying to gain a short-term loan from the city by refusing to pay their taxes; hence reducing the grace period would make delaying payment unprofitable. In 1968, for example, the city's penalty for delinquent taxes was 7 percent per year, while the interest rate charged by most banks was 9 percent (*New York Times*, November, 13, 1968). When facing the possible loss of their property, city officials reasoned, most landlords would pay their tax liability promptly.

What these officials failed to realize was that non-payment of taxes by property owners was a last-ditch, strategic move and not just a tactical one. Most of the delinquent properties were in declining neighborhoods that had lost much of their value in the 1960s and 1970s. As middle and upper middle income tenants left the city for the suburbs or other regions, entrepreneurs were left with a reduced demand and a much poorer clientele. As market rent levels fell, property values fell, too. The city's tax assessors, however, were very slow in lowering assessments.

The lack of rental income and the high property tax burden led many already delinquent owners to adopt strategies of disinvestment. Such a strategy would involve making only minimally necessary repairs and maintenance expenditures and putting off the city's tax collectors for as long as possible. Thus reducing the grace period but not the overall tax liability forced entrepreneurs who could not (or would not) pay to forfeit properties at an accelerated rate.

The 1977 "fast foreclosure" law, which reduced the grace period to one year, led to a modest decrease in the property tax delinquency rate and a rapid takeover of properties by the city. From 1974 to 1979, the number of residential properties in city ownership rose from 4,367 to 13,034. Most of this increase came from walk-up apartment buildings in the older boroughs of the city: Brooklyn, Manhattan, and the Bronx.

Just as important as the fast foreclosure policy were major changes in the city's disposition policy. The auctioning off of abandoned in rem properties came under increasing attack as auctioned properties found their way back into the city's hands. For several years, the city had a moratorium on sales of in rem properties. So with the escape valve on the in rem system closed, the inventory rose to its present levels.

While some 6,000 of these 10,000 in rem buildings have been completely abandoned by their owners and emptied of their tenants, their doors and windows sealed, the remaining 4,000 in rem buildings contain some 48,000 occupied apartments and 5,000 vacant ones. The total number of units in the in rem stock is unknowable, however, since the city never made a precise count of the apartments in the vacant buildings before they were sealed. The best estimate available is that another 70,000 potential apartments are in the 6,000 unoccupied buildings.

"Housing New York" Plan

In May 1985, Governor Cuomo and Mayor Koch announced a $4.2 billion *Housing New York* Program to produce low and moderate income housing largely by rehabilitating the existing in rem stock. Since then, the program's total costs have soared to $5.2 billion, some $4.4 billion of which is to come from purely local sources (Berenyi, 1989).

Despite its name, however, *Housing New York* is less a new housing program that a plan to repackage and expand the city's existing programs. The purpose of *Housing New York* is to divert as much of the city's and state's newly available capital funds as possible into housing rehabilitation. The city often makes it appear that these funds are irretrievably designated for housing rehabilitation and that other alternatives are not feasible; however, the degree to which these funds are truly "surplus" and the efficacy of putting them into city-sponsored in rem rehabilitation is questionable. Three chief sources of these "surplus" funds are the city's Community Development Block Grant (CDBG) from the federal government, funds from the city's Municipal Assistance Corporation, and the city's revenues from the Battery Park City Authority. The CDBG funds are, in essence, revenue sharing funds from the federal government, which can be used for a variety of local development purposes. While these funds are designated for projects such as the in rem rehabs, the other two surplus funds are better described as general revenue to the city.

The Battery Park City Authority, proposed by Governor Rockefeller to create a landfill redevelopment area on the Hudson River waterfront in downtown Manhattan, has proved to be a financial gold mine for city and state government. The authority was permitted to issue bonds to construct the landfill site, and while the buildings in Battery Park City are all privately constructed and privately owned, the authority has retained title to the land and is receiving revenue from the lease of this land. The revenue from these land leases, especially from the World Financial Center, greatly exceeds the authority's debt service and amortization costs, and the authority has signed an agreement with the governor allowing the state to issue tax exempt bonds backed by these surplus revenues to be used for the rehabilitation of the city's in rem housing (Settlement Housing Fund Inc., 1987).

The Municipal Assistance Corporation (MAC) has a much different history, inspired less by a vision of a city of shining office towers than by the nightmare of metropolitan bankruptcy and decay. During the fiscal crisis, Governor Hugh Carey established the MAC to convert the city's burgeoning short-term debt into less expensive long-term debt. Because the nation's investment community feared that the city would default on its bonds, the state had to step in to provide a new guarantee to the city's credit worthiness.

Because of the state's guarantee and its priority claim on the city's sales tax revenue, MAC bonds were able to command a much lower interest rate than the city could on its own. Because of its lower interest rate, MAC was able to sell its bonds and buy the city's debt at a profit.

Under the current system, the MAC board of directors under the chairmanship of financier Felix Rohatyn has a certain control over the allocation of the city's sales tax revenue and the "profits" from MAC bond sales, allowing many of the city's financial decisions to be taken out of the usual budget process. Beginning in December 1984, Rohatyn and the MAC board were persuaded to use these MAC profits to rehabilitate the city's in rem housing stock (Settlement Housing Fund Inc., 1987).

In this way, the Housing New York Program treats the surplus Battery Park City money and the surplus MAC funds as "found" money.

According to this view, found money should not be compared with other city expenditures. Found money is new money that city officials have earned through wise investment and should spend on their favorite new project. New money should not be put into the general treasury, used to pay off old debts, or used to reduce the city's tax burden; new money should be used on new projects.

The danger of this thinking is that the city's normal, less politically exciting capital and maintenance needs are being neglected. New York City desperately needs better maintenance and capital improvements in its road, transit, water, and sewer systems. By dedicating revenue sources to its housing program the city shortchanges its other service needs. The more overarching problem with the *Housing New York* Program is that New York City, unlike any other city in the country, will become a housing-rehabilitation conglomerate, in the process further distorting its private housing market. A recent report commissioned by the city's Department of Housing, Preservation, and Development, looking at locally funded housing production or rehabilitation programs in the fifty-one largest cities in the United States, noted that, by every available category of measurement, New York had the largest such program in the country (Berenyi, 1989). Not only did New York spend the largest amount of money of any of the fifty cities, but the city had the highest per capita rate of spending and overall *spent three times more than all the other cities combined.*[4]

If these dollars were all that public housing cost the city, public housing would still be an inefficient response to the problem of low income housing. As we shall see, however, the price of the city's heavy investment in public housing involves far more than this immediate dollar outlay.

The Price of the Public Housing Monopoly

New York's large public housing sector imposes at least four other significant costs, beyond the city's staggering budgetary expenditures. It deprives the city of property tax revenue, it competes with privately owned, low and moderate cost housing, it is profoundly unfair in its distribution of benefits to the eligible poor, and it exacerbates welfare dependency.

Since housing owned by the public and the non-profit sectors is not subject to the property tax, an added cost of New York City's reliance on publicly funded housing is a reduction in revenue. Every expansion of the public housing supply that displaces privately owned property shrinks the city's property tax base without reducing the demand for city services, and requires higher property tax rates on the rest of the tax base, discouraging new housing investment and spurring housing abandonment.

Much more harmful to the housing market in low and moderate income neighborhoods is the role of publicly owned or subsidized housing in competing with the unsubsidized private housing sector. Even though most public involvement is justified as offering decent housing for families too poor to afford private housing, in fact all public sector providers: The New York City Housing Authority, the Mitchell-Lama operators and the non-profit sponsors of *Housing New York* have been aggressively recruiting the most affluent and stable of those nominally eligible as tenants. These are the very families who could afford the less expensive private sector apartments, and whom private landlords in these areas desperately wish to retain. At the same time they often turn away, when they can (an increasingly difficult task under federal rules and local housing exigencies), the poorest and most troubled households. Thus, the private sector is often left to house precisely the families whose behavior problems make them the least suitable tenants, and whose low income insures they will occupy the most deteriorated apartments. Of course, the consequences of this policy inversion—public housing for the stable, near poor, and private housing for the troubled and indigent—becomes further proof that the private sector is incapable of serving any but the middle class and the rich, justifying further expansion of the public housing sector.

But even from the perspective of the present and potential tenants of public housing, the growth of New York City's public housing sector has involved costs as well as benefits. For those lucky enough to receive or inherit an apartment in one or another segment of the public housing stock, the low rents and relatively high housing quality cannot be matched. Rents in these projects are well below the prevailing market rates, and the oldest provider, the New York City Housing Authority has been fastidious about maintaining its buildings and selecting responsible (that is, non-poor) tenants (at least compared to housing authorities in other cities). Yet to attain this benefit, prospective public housing tenants have to wait many years on the Housing Authority's or HPD's waiting lists, currently some 170,000 names long, or engage in one or another demeaning stratagem. And if tenants are unhappy about the size or quality of their apartments, they have few places to turn. With rents below the market rate for comparable private units, the Housing Authority, HPD, or other non-profit providers have very little decent quality competition (the consequence of undermining the private low-cost housing market).

Thus, in terms of equity or fairness, New York's public housing functions as a lottery, much in the same way that rent regulation does. Benefits accrue to those who wait years for an apartment, those who have been in the system a very long time, or those who move along the fast track by declaring themselves homeless. The large majority of the poor are never served, all the more so because, as indicated, the NYCHA and HPD have consciously tried to keep a mix of income groups within the public housing sector that reserves no more than half of all public units for the truly poor.

Finally, to the extent that the policy of basing rents on income levels has made public housing more of an income maintenance program than a housing program, it must be evaluated in connection with other forms of welfare. Like all forms of welfare, public housing creates a disincentive to work and fosters dependency. For example, in most public housing (not including Mitchell-Lama) rent is calculated at 30 percent of a household's income. For every extra $100 in reported income earned, an extra $30 in rent may be charged. This 30 percent rule acts as an implicit 30 percent tax rate, above and beyond the federal, state, and city income tax and the Social Security tax. If a household is a multiple program beneficiary receiving food stamps, AFDC or home relief, and/or Medicaid, each with its separate implicit tax rate, it may face a tax rate well over 100 percent. This creates enormous disincentives to work or truthfully report income. Of course, this is a more general problem of all welfare programs.

Changing Course

The city should, as quickly as possible, implement a policy that will return its tax-foreclosed buildings to private hands. All properties sold to new private owners must also be promised reasonable tax assessments and tax rates, so they will not be forced into tax foreclosure again. Even reasonable tax rates will generate extra income for the city. Sales contracts should also exempt building owners from future rent controls. For privatized buildings in prospering neighborhoods, a steady demand of moderate to middle income tenants should guarantee a sufficiently large potential rent roll for developers to want to buy them. Some buyers might even find demand sufficient to replace existing structures and to construct new residential buildings.

In more marginal neighborhoods, buyers might have to struggle to find a use for their properties. But the cycle of abandonment could be broken if the city removed previous tax liabilities and let owners choose a site's best use, whether as a cooperative conversion, as a middle income rental building, or possibly even as a low cost commercial use such as a parking lot. In comparison to the city's current policy of holding on to dormant, vacant buildings, just about any other use would be more profitable to the city treasury and less damaging to the surrounding neighborhoods. What the city should *not* do is to continue to develop these properties itself or give them away to private and non-profit developers with heavy loan subsidies and minimal private equity stakes.

In today's context, a greatly expanded and rehabilitated in rem stock will mean a constant demand for operating subsidies. Where will the city's source of operating subsidies come from at the end of the ten-year *Housing New York* plan? The city has entered a brave new world in making these commitments, but it will not be able to follow through.

That the city should find itself facing such commitments at all is perhaps the single greatest legacy of its tradition of public housing leadership. What in other cities might be viewed as evidence of excessive government spending, or an unusual extension of governmental activities, New York City officials consider a badge of honor. Unlike any other city, New York has adopted the housing ideology of government-sponsored development as the only means of solving its citizens' housing needs.

This ideology, in turn, has created a convenient scapegoat for local politicians, whose commitment to construct more public housing is considered the crucial litmus test among tenant activists and the city's poor. Whenever state or federal funding for public housing is threatened or reduced, local politicians are shielded from a candid examination of their housing policies. And as more buildings and more vacant land have been taken over by the public sector, the likelihood of either the private market or the public sector successfully meeting the housing crisis is diminished.

10

The State of the Debate

In addressing what everyone agrees is a scarcity of vacant housing at affordable rents, city politicians face a dilemma. In the short term, they have an incentive to favor incumbent tenants by restraining rent increases; in the long term, they realize rent regulations must be curtailed if new housing is to be built. The politician as tenant champion and redistributionist proposes extending rent regulation to unregulated apartments, broadening of lease-succession and tenure rights, capping MCI increases for run-down properties, and means-testing rent control for poor tenants in stabilized units. The politician who views developers and landlords as agents of growth advocates vacancy decontrol for gentrifying areas, luxury decontrol for Manhattan, and raising the rate of allowable rent increases under MCI. This tenant-redistributionist/landlord-growth dialectic is sensitive to a pragmatic calculus of votes to be won or lost, and results in inefficient half-measures and minor adjustments in the rent-regulatory system. Together with the excessive reliance on public housing, it precludes any principled, efficient, market-oriented policy to address the city's housing scarcity.

Regulating the Unregulated

The first item on the redistributionist agenda is to broaden the scope of rent regulation to cover all housing units in the city. As table 10.1 shows, 517,000 New York City households, or one quarter of all renters, live in private apartments not covered by either of the two main rent-regulation programs, and they bear the full brunt of changes in the city's housing market. These apartments fall into three main groups: units in buildings of fewer than six total, post-1974 apartments that did not receive tax abatements, and sublets of condo and co-op apartments.

The largest of these categories, units in small buildings, is probably safe from rent stabilization for powerful political and administrative reasons. Many of these small buildings, placed under rent control in 1942, were decontrolled upon a change in tenancy, so that only 19,774 remain in the older program.

The administrative costs of regulating the city's one-, two-, and three-family homes would be astronomical, greatly multiplying the number of financial records that would need to be kept and audited. Moreover, regulating small buildings makes no political sense at all given the ratio of tenants to landlords. What politician would lever-age his constituency by offending one property owner just to benefit one or two tenants?

Table 10.1.   Unregulated apartments, 1986[a]

Decontrolled units	
In bldgs. with fewer than 6 units	254,433
Condo/co-op rentals	721
Larger or not reported	12,742
Total decontrolled	267,896
Other rental housing	
In bldgs. with fewer than 6 units	147,327
Condo/co-op rentals	37,263
Larger or not reported	119,635
Total other	304,225
Total	572,121

Source: U.S. Bureau of the Census, 1987.

a. Buildings of fewer than six units may have a small overlap with condo/co-op rentals. The "other rental" category does include in rem housing and some SROs, as well as unregulated, privately owned units. The net number of unregulated apartments, properly adjusted by subtracting 5,000 SROs and 50,000 in rem units from the total, is thus 517,000.

Furthermore, the outer borough homeowner who rents out his upstairs or basement apartment or the landlord who actually lives in his own apartment building is looked upon as a cultural hero to much of the voting public. The homeowner-landlord is a small businessman and community institution, and as such is politically untouchable.

These unregulated apartments form an important part of the housing stock in the city's quasi-suburban sections in the outer boroughs. In Staten Island, for example, 64.3 percent of the housing stock consists of unregulated rentals. Other less regulated areas include Southern Queens, 53.9 percent; Northwest Queens, 51.1 percent; Northeast Bronx, 41.3 percent; and South Brooklyn, 38.7 percent.

Apartments in post-1974 unsubsidized buildings, on the other hand, are somewhat more vulnerable to new regulation. They have escaped so far only because, under the Emergency Tenant Protection Act of 1974, an apartment built without benefit of any tax abatements or subsidies escapes rent regulation. With available data it is difficult to determine the precise number of unregulated post-1974 rental units, but our best estimate is approximately 75,000.[1] Whether these apartments will remain unregulated will be a test of the state legislature's credibility. Given the legislature's record to date, as discussed in chapter 6, one can hardly expect these buildings to escape rent regulation forever.

The threat of new regulation appears most imminent, however, with respect to the 38,000 condominium or cooperative apartments that are rented out by their individual owners. Ironically, the condo/co-op market was developed in part as a means to evade rent regulations. Because rent stabilization does not allow market rents to be charged upon vacancy, the best way for an owner of a regulated rental building to capture its full market value is through conversion to co-op or condominium ownership.

Because regulated apartments are valuable to their occupants, the state legislature has tightened the rules governing conversion plans that permit eviction of existing tenants. In response, owners have adopted non-eviction plans that allow incumbent renters to remain in their apartment after the conversion. As a result, a converted apartment building will typically have a jumbled mixture of tenants and owners.

Under a non-eviction plan, state regulations *require* a minimum number of apartments to be sold for a plan to be declared "effective." To reach this minimum, the converter must often offer incumbent tenants a below-market purchase price to entice them to switch from tenant to owner. In effect, these discounts or "insider prices" are legalized bribes designed to remove the apartment from rent regulation, and indeed many tenants buy their apartments at "insider prices" and then, in a practice known as "flipping," sell them right away at a higher market price.

The incumbent tenant may choose not to accept the insider discount, and instead remain in the building indefinitely, paying his below-market rent, so that full conversion of a rental building may take an entire generation, or not occur at all.

The growing number of condo and co-op converted buildings—with their idiosyncratic mixture of owners who are tenants, owners who are investors, regulated tenants, and unregulated tenants—is generating a virulent mixture of castelike legal inequalities, confusions about responsibilities for building maintenance, and concomitant jealousies between tenured and untenured tenants all literally living under the same roof. As long as conversion and the ownership market remain the only avenue for owners to recoup the full value of their property, the number of unregulated condo tenants will grow.

With the rest of the housing market so tightly regulated, tenants in these unregulated apartments face the full brunt of any shortage or glut on the rental housing market. As the unregulated sector grows, these tenants may form a larger political constituency, either for broadening the scope of rent regulation, or—if they recognize the harm the system is causing them—for reducing regulation.

Means-Tested Rent Control

Interestingly, there is one redistributionist idea not on the tenant agenda that seems alluring: a means test for rent regulation, to insure that only the poorest tenants are protected from paying market rents.

Although this proposal is usually put forward by landlords and has been fiercely resisted by tenant activists, the intention of the measure would be to redistribute the benefits of rent regulation. Under such a proposal, tenants would have to submit evidence of income annually to DHCR, which would determine the allowable rent increase. In fact, a similar system already exists in the city's Senior Citizen Rent Increase Exemption Program (SCRIE); under this program, a low income senior citizen in a regulated apartment submits an annual income statement and is protected from paying more than 30 percent of his or her income. If the regulated rent exceeds that amount, the landlord is reimbursed by a corresponding reduction in his property tax.

One possible scenario for means testing would thus be the extension of SCRIE to all age groups in the city. But if this were done, the cost to the city in lost property taxes would be prohibitive. At present, SCRIE has a very low participation rate and a small cost in lost revenue. An alternative to a property-tax-funded means test for rent control would be an unfunded means-tested system, operating as the current rent-regulation system does, which does not compensate owners. Under such a system, however, landlords would have a strong incentive to exclude the poor from their apartments to avoid future rents from being constrained. A system funded by landlords would need monitoring of landlords to prevent harassment of existing poor tenants, since removing them would be rewarded with a rent increase.

Clearly, then, any scheme of landlord-funded rent control that is means-tested could only work as a transitional system that grandfathered existing low income tenants, thereby sidestepping the issue of tenant selection. This said, means testing could be used as a method to correct past regulatory distortions and start a new system of regulation or to phase-in an unregulated housing market. Of course, the question of what kind of housing system would *follow* the transition would be open-ended.

Alas, an unfunded, means-tested rent-regulation system may not even be constitutional. In the recent case of *Pennell* v. *San Jose*, the Supreme Court upheld San Jose's means-tested rent-regulation statute, but on the grounds that a specific landlord-tenant dispute had not been brought to the Court. The substance of whether means-tested rent control is a constitutional taking has not yet been decided by the Supreme Court.

Vacancy Decontrol

The proposal most often advanced by the pro-growth forces is vacancy decontrol, under which vacant apartments may be rented at
market levels to new tenants. One proposed form of vacancy decontrol would return the city to the pre-1974 system, under which vacant apartments were allowed to capture a market return and thereafter be permanently decontrolled. Another variant, similar to the
system in Los Angeles and many other cities, would allow rents to be
set by rent stabilization, but with annual increases pegged to the
general inflation rate, and full market-rate catch-ups at each change
in tenancy.

Redistributionists frequently object to vacancy decontrol on the
grounds that it would decrease the supply of low and moderate income housing. This objection assumes, however, that the below-
market rent apartments are currently being occupied by low income
tenants. As we have seen, many middle and upper income tenants
preempt the below-market apartments, either because such tenants
have better connections and better information about apartment vacancies, or because existing tenants in regulated buildings are given
first dibs at vacant units.

Redistributionists also protest that vacancy decontrol would create an incentive for landlords to harass their tenants to generate
higher turnover. This objection cannot be easily dismissed. Certainly,
a host of harassment cases have been brought to court in the last few
years, and unscrupulous landlords have even been shown to invite
loud musicians, drug addicts, pit bulls, and thugs into their buildings
as a means of driving current tenants out. Other owners appear to
have deliberately reduced maintenance and security to achieve the
same end.

Still, it must be remembered that such harassment is endemic to
any rent-control system. Under rent regulation, the landlord assumes that he could *always do better* with another tenant who would
be willing to pay the same amount or more. If a tenant leaves, many
other tenants would be eager to take his place. The tenant, on the
other hand, knows that to get a similar apartment elsewhere he
would *certainly do worse*, either finding a lesser apartment for the
same price or having to pay more. Thus while vacancy decontrol
might in fact increase harassment over the short term, in the long

run it would decrease the number of regulated units, reducing harassment incentives.

Luxury Decontrol

After vacancy decontrol, the second most common proposal on the pro-growth agenda is a form of deregulation that was written into the original rent-control statutes of the 1940s and 1950s. Under this program, rent control was lifted for any "class" of apartments for which the vacancy rate had risen above 5 percent. Since the most expensive classes of apartments tended to have the highest vacancy rates, this measure became known as "luxury decontrol."

The basic premise of luxury decontrol is that anyone who lives in an expensive apartment must be so rich as not to need the protection of rent regulation. In this sense, luxury decontrol is essentially a form of means testing. However, just as it it would be incorrect to assume that the rich do not occupy low-rent apartments, so it would be incorrect to assume that high-rent apartments are occupied only by the rich.

Newly formed households, for instance, as well as families or individuals who have only recently moved into the city, are generally forced to compete in the housing market at much higher rent levels than everyone else. They usually cannot afford long searches for low-rent, stabilized apartments, nor do they often have the contacts needed to find them. Because of this mismatch of rents and household incomes, any luxury decontrol proposal would affect households of all incomes, not just the rich.

Luxury decontrol would also "protect" households of all incomes—low income households in poor neighborhoods as well as high income households benefiting from rent control. Ultimately, any luxury-decontrol plan must reflect the inequality of current rent distortions.

In any case, luxury decontrol might not be a politically viable solution. Even when the rent-regulation statutes included luxury decontrol provisions, the city was reluctant to enforce them. Under the decontrol rules of the 1950s and 1960s, landlords were forced to sue the city to obtain decontrol when the vacancy rate for certain groups of apartments rose above 5 percent. More recently, when confronted with 1987 vacancy rates of 5.9 percent for apartments renting between $750 and $999 and 6.9 percent for those above $1,000, the Rent Stabilization Association appealed to the city to implement luxury decontrol, and the city council refused (*New York Times,* March 13, 1988, and March 23, 1988; *New York Newsday,* March 23, 1988).

Major Capital Improvements (MCIs)

Under New York's MCI system, landlords make improvements and then request from the State Department of Housing and Community Renewal increases in the base rent to compensate them for their expenditures. Under DHCR's current rules, if the agency approves an increase (and this can take years), a landlord can increase the monthly rent by one sixtieth of the amount of the "reasonable cost" of the improvement, up to a 6 percent ceiling. The reasonable-cost provision means DHCR is supposed to check whether the owner is making truly necessary repairs and is reporting the correct cost. The improvement would then be paid off in five years. After the five-year "repayment period," the MCI increase becomes part of the rent base upon which all future rent increases are calculated, which in theory represents the landlord's profit.

Tenant activists have strongly criticized the permanent increase in the base rent as a windfall to the landlord, whereas spokesmen for the owners have predictably defended it. Who is right?

In practice, a landlord's profit is much smaller than it might appear. First, the five-year "repayment period" does not actually "repay" an investment. For example, no one would make a $100 investment today simply to receive one hundred dollars next year (or for that matter, five years from now). If we assume a 10 percent cost of borrowing *and no risk,* a minimum return of $110 must be offered one year from now to attract $100 today. Similarly, $121 must be offered two years from now or $161 in five years to attract a $100 investment.[2]

Second, any landlord making an MCI takes a risk that a rent increase will be denied by either the DHCR administrators or the tenants. An administrator may choose to deny the increase or simply to delay its implementation. DHCR spokesmen admit that processing MCI applications currently takes 12 to 15 months (*New York Times,* April 24, 1988). For a necessary repair that cannot be delayed, this processing time will cost the landlord one or more years of interest and eat away at his investment return. Delaying the repairs while awaiting approval may worsen the problem and extend the damage. Even if an MCI is approved by the DHCR, tenants may be unwilling or unable to accept the rent increase.

The proper way to assess the current MCI system is to calculate the value of the return, which in this case is the increase in rent. Calculating the present value of an MCI is similar to the previous example, only instead of a single payment of $110 or $121, we have a series of small monthly payments over a number of years. Using a little algebra and some assumptions about future rent increases and interest rates, we can calculate the total present value of this stream of rent increases.[3]

An analysis of such present value calculations shows that under prevailing interest rates, rent increases beyond five years are necessary to make any investment profitable.[4] Then again, if the payments extend indefinitely, all investments will be profitable, up to some arbitrary dollar figure based upon the monthly rent.

Given the risks and uncertain gains of present MCI rules, a proposal of the landlord advocates would uncap the 6 percent MCI ceiling. But the problem with any MCI program, whatever the ceiling, is that any improvement must be assessed and approved by a bureaucrat, not by a consumer, that is, the tenant. An MCI program thus forces tenants to pay higher rents whether or not landlords actually improve the building to their liking.

Another difficulty is that the public regulatory authority must investigate every investment for appropriateness. In the city of New York there are thousands of landlords and literally millions of apartments, each of which will eventually need new boilers, new roofs, new windows, and so forth. Inspecting that many apartments and collecting sufficient information to judge each expenditure is something of which *no* regulatory authority or central planning agency is capable. DHCR spokesmen admit that processing MCI applications currently takes 12 to 15 months, but in fact it often takes longer (*New York Times*, April 24, 1988). For a landlord who is making a necessary repair that cannot be delayed, this processing time will cost him one or more years of interest and will eat away at his investment return. Not repairing the building while awaiting this approval may exacerbate this damage.

The fundamental problem with the MCI system, in short, is that in trying to assess improvements it is trying to do the impossible. The only mechanism that can efficiently assess the worthiness of any improvement is the market in which tenants and landlords assess the value of individual apartments. To choose between higher or lower MCI ceilings is to accept a false alternative. The answer is to replace ad-hoc MCI reimbursements with the principles of market discipline.

What Next for Mitchell-Lama?

Another contentious issue dividing the tenant and landlord camps is the fate of Mitchell-Lama apartments (see chapter 6), which are slated to be freed from regulations if they were built more than 20 years ago. The state legislature is currently considering a bill that would extend the deregulation threshold to 35 years and retroactively apply it to projects built under the 20-year agreement. The bill also proposes an increase in the allowable owners' profit margin from 6 to 8.5 percent, providing some additional funds for repair and maintenance, extending the permissible period of tax exemption from 20 to 30 years, and phasing in higher surcharges for over-income tenants. These changes are designed primarily to cloak the attempted betrayal as a "comprehensive reform" and thus increase the bill's chance of passage.

Legislators and tenant activists have asserted that New York is on the verge of a housing Armageddon. Yet the owners who are seeking to remove their buildings from the Mitchell-Lama program have stipulated their willingness to become subject to rent stabilization at their existing low rent levels. In the event of subsequent cooperative or condominium conversion, the housing companies have further consented to use only non-eviction plans, in which all non-purchasing households are free to remain as rent-regulated tenants. Given these responsible, extra-contractual concessions, the prospect of mass evictions and increased homelessness that tenant advocates fear is highly unlikely.

Toward a Housing Policy

The various debates that define New York's current housing policy are like blows from a grudge match whose original cause has long been forgotten. The dispute feeds upon itself. Rents are frozen, apartments deteriorate, and a formula is adopted to encourage investment. The argument is over the formula, not the freeze. Rents are frozen, tenants share their apartments, and the original tenant dies. The lawyers fight over the inheritance, not questioning the freeze. Rents are frozen, owners convert rentals to ownership, and a mechanism is devised to determine when conversion can take place. The political issue is the mechanism, not the freeze.

Because of the complexity of the legislation, the variety of responses by landlords and tenants to the legislation, and the multitude of unintended consequences, each of which requires further regulation, New York's housing policy has become segmented into dozens of separate issues. Candidates and public officials prepare issue papers or position statements, each of which is calibrated to attract the marginal voters who care most about that aspect of the legislation: MCI caps for tenants in run-down properties, vacancy decontrol for landlords in gentrifying areas, means-tested rent control for poor tenants in stabilized apartments, or luxury decontrol for Manhattan landlords.

The sum of these many little debates, however, does not a housing policy make. In the next chapter, therefore, we propose a policy for replacing the existing patchwork of regulations and stop-gap measures with a comprehensive market-oriented solution.

11

Abundance by Design

Proper Allocation of the Housing Stock

A fundamental reform of New York's housing policies must involve sending the right price signals to its housing market. This elementary concept is most salient in the realm of rent regulation, but it also affects rent regulation's housing policy handmaidens: land use regulation, property tax assessment, and housing subsidies. Like all other consumer goods and and services, housing is a scarce and valued commodity. Ideally, housing should be distributed among all potential households efficiently and equitably. There is no way to do this in New York or anywhere else without depending on the role of prices. We need housing prices (sales prices and rents) set freely in the housing market according to the desirability and value of each dwelling. The only way to do this is through the dynamics of supply and demand.

In an unregulated market, buyers and renters would naturally value large apartments more than small ones, and apartments with particular amenities such as scenic views, larger rooms, or elevators more than those without them. When apartments in different locations around the city share identical characteristics, then apartments in better (more attractive, safer, more prestigious) neighborhoods would tend to be more expensive than those in less desirable areas. Apartments close to midtown Manhattan would be valued higher than ones further away. There might be *apparent* anomalies and irrationalities in the distribution of rents, but these would be tested periodically by the market, would be freely determined by consumer demand, and would likely reflect those subtle and subjective apartment characteristics that casual outside observers might not catch or be able to quantify.

Only if we allow the prices and rents of New York's housing stock to be set naturally by the market will housing in New York be rationally, efficiently, and, for the first time in forty years, *fairly* distributed. Under market-based pricing, small families in large apartments would no longer pay lower rents than large families in small ones. Households in Manhattan would no longer pay less for nice apartments than households in the Bronx pay for squalid ones. Residents of identical apartments in a Manhattan high rise would no longer pay wildly disparate rents. Most important, the rich would no longer pay as little or less for their housing as the poor—unless they were willing to live in squalid or cramped apartments.

Of course, the specter of market-priced housing has always provoked resistance from entrenched beneficiaries of price controls, as well as from the idealistic, the socially conscious, or the merely misinformed. It is typically alleged that housing would cost more for the lower and middle classes, causing wholesale displacement of families with modest means and swelling the ranks of homeless. Contrary to such nightmare scenarios, market-priced housing would actually *increase* the opportunities for the less affluent families of New York to find affordable housing—*even in the absence of any new construction or rehabilitation of additional housing.* But construction and rehabilitation would indeed take place, because a housing market with market-based prices would encourage new housing construction.

Furthermore, it can hardly be the case that the effects of price decontrol would be visited primarily on lower and middle income groups. After all, as we observed in Chapter 2, the primary beneficiaries of rent regulation are well-to-do residents of Manhattan.

Still, as we shall shortly see, deregulation can be designed to protect the poorest tenants during a transitional period. And even if market-priced housing should turn out to be beyond the reach of the poorest families, carefully targeted subsidies for such households would in any case be cheaper and far more efficient than the scattershot effects of the present system.

Finally, even if the entire private housing sector in New York City were subject to market prices, public agencies would still control over 200,000 units of housing, which could house those families unable to find decent market-priced apartments.

Let there be no mistaking it: the path to a healthy housing market must involve the eventual *end* of the city's system of price controls. We are not talking about revising or reforming the rules of rent control and rent stabilization, but rather their total elimination, as well as strong legislative barriers to their reimposition.

The reason for taking such an extreme position is simple. Even a benign and mild form of rent regulation—that is, one that guarantees owners a fair return and is replete with procedural safeguards—would set out to achieve an objective that is subversive to a proper allocation of the city's housing supply. Any form of rent regulation, however mild, is intended to depress rents below present or future market levels. But any discrepancy between natural and regulated rent creates serious distortions in the housing market, and massive misallocations of the housing stock.

The Transition

The road to market-priced housing for New York City is conceptually easy but politically difficult. For this reason, the transition from a system of regulated to market-determined prices must be designed to protect the most vulnerable tenants for a certain length of time. There are any number of ways to achieve this.

The most gradual transition formula (and thus the method that would diffuse the benefits of deregulation over the longest period of time) would be vacancy decontrol. All apartments would remain regulated until their present tenants voluntarily moved out or died. For vacancy decontrol to be effective at all, regulatory protection would *not* be extended to relatives or friends of the statutory tenants or leaseholders other than spouses. Vacancy decontrol would shield the entire tenantry of New York City from any real or perceived harm from deregulation during the transitional period, and thus should be politically the most palatable transition scheme. However, vacancy decontrol would represent a very slow transition to a completely unregulated private housing market, taking perhaps twenty years to run its course.

Another transitional concept would relate the speed of deregulation to the incomes and the "vulnerability" of tenants. All households in unregulated apartments would have to furnish documentation of their income to the official rent regulatory agency, the New York State Division of Housing and Community Renewal (DHCR). During a five-year transitional period, rents could rise to a level representing 25 percent of gross monthly income, but could increase by no more than, say, 10 percent, in any year during the transition. In the sixth year, all apartments would be fully deregulated. Such a scheme could be modified in a number of ways. Any of the parameters could be changed: the transition period could be longer than five years; the rent-income ratio could be lower than 25 percent (or variable by income class); or the annual increment could be more or less than 10 percent.

A further modification would be to blend the income-based transitional plan with the vacancy-decontrol idea. Apartments currently housing certain classes of tenants—namely, the elderly and the poor—could be subject to the vacancy-decontrol plan only, while apartments with younger and wealthier tenants would be subject to the time-limited decontrol. We are sure that many other transitional concepts, or variants on our proposals, could be devised by the ingenuity of the New York State legislature. The important thing is to move to total deregulation.

Build More Housing

Enormous benefits to New York's housing would attend deregulation as much of the existing stock were freed up and all of it were better maintained. Even greater benefits would accrue once developers built rental housing in New York City again, especially if they were to build—as they once did—moderately priced housing for middle income families in the boroughs outside Manhattan. How do we get this to happen?

Let us begin by saying what we are *not* proposing. We are confident that it would be unnecessary (and undesirable) to offer builders subsidies, free land, tax abatements, or no-money-down, discount-rate financing. Decontrol by itself would breathe new life into the construction of rental housing. No longer would discount-priced, regulated apartments be competing with market-priced new ones. No longer would the present value of new rental dwellings be depressed by the prospect of rent regulation in the future. Decontrol would send a signal to the development community that New York

City and New York State once again appreciate the contribution of the private sector in meeting the city's enormous housing needs.

But the pace of new housing construction can be guided by other measures besides decontrol of prices in the rental market.

Reform the Zoning Laws

More land must be freed up in New York City to accommodate new housing construction. This means that the city's land use regulations must be made more hospitable. Vast areas of land currently zoned for manufacturing activities that will never materialize must be rezoned to permit housing. Many areas of the city, especially outside of central Manhattan, that are zoned for artificially low housing densities must be rezoned to permit more housing, to strike a proper balance between the prevailing character of these neighborhoods and the need for more housing.

The Uniform Land Use Review Procedure (ULURP) must be transformed from a vehicle that blocks new housing construction to one that—as it was originally intended—expedites development. The problem with ULURP is not so much in the time clock running once a project is officially in the ULURP process, but the many months or years it takes to get into the ULURP process, the so-called precertification period. To speed certification of projects, other layers of regulatory requirements must be eliminated or streamlined.

Finally, a great deal of land could be made available for new housing if the city and state sold some of their holdings. The city owns untold acres of land underneath its vacant in rem housing stock. The 580-odd miles of city waterfront represent a largely untapped land resource with thousands of acres owned by the city, state, and federal governments.

To repeat: we are not proposing any subsidies whatever. Whether the land is owned privately or publicly, we expect builders to pay prevailing market prices for it—and still be able to offer new apartments and houses at a wide range of prices and rents.

Overhaul the Property Tax Code

The market for new housing would be further invigorated by a rational system of property taxes. The present system is entirely the product of narrow political calculations. Apartment houses bear a much higher effective rate of taxation than one-, two-, or even three-family homes. Manhattan properties are taxed at higher effective rates than those in the outer boroughs, and properties in New York's poorer neighborhoods are taxed more heavily than affluent areas. Since the tax burden on rental property is passed through to tenants as part of the rent, the skewed property tax system makes new rental housing development less economically viable, especially if it is located in one of the city's less desirable neighborhoods.

The amount of these tax differentials can be quite significant. An equalization of the tax burden would not only mean more affordable housing, but would spur construction of moderately priced units.

Free up Public Housing

Even though the public sector comprises only between 6 and 14 percent of the city's housing inventory (depending on one's definition of "public"), it plays an important role in the overall dynamics of the housing market. Since there are several different types of public housing programs, our recommendations are tailored to each.

First off, there is no need for public agencies to compete with the private sector for middle income tenants. The presumed need for a public presence (through subsidy or outright ownership) in the middle-priced housing market niche is a myth, based either on political exigency or a misreading of facts. Virtually all tenants of middle income subsidized housing, such as the 15,000 households of Co-op City in the Bronx, could find housing in New York's private housing sector. Alternatively, Co-op City could charge market "rents" (co-op maintenance charges in actuality) without visiting any hardship on the majority of its residents.

Thus we recommend that *all* shallow-subsidy, publicly sponsored housing in New York City be "privatized" and sold or rented at market prices. The details of this transfer to private ownership and the pricing of this sector would depend on the characteristics of each affected development. Some developments are already slated to move out from under the umbrella of shallow-subsidy restrictions and rent regulation. All that needs to be done is not to impede the schedule.

In the case of Mitchell-Lama cooperative dwellings such as those in Co-op City, the apartments are already "owned" by their residents. All that is needed is to make cooperative ownership a market-based reality rather than a sham. Such dwelling units would lose their considerable New York State subsidy, which holds down maintenance costs; management would be turned over to the cooperative shareholders, and all restrictions would be removed regarding the terms and prices that their owners could charge upon resale. Present owners might be asked to "buy out" the New York State agency for a modest sum to reimburse New York State for two decades of subsidies and to reduce the potential equity windfall.

Any disgruntlement that higher monthly expenses might provoke among subsidized co-op owners should be mitigated by the large equity windfall that would remain after the removal of resale constraints. In the case of middle income rental developments such as Starrett City, the present not-for-profit ownership entities would be required to sell the developments to private for-profit corporations, with the proceeds going to New York State in consideration of the cost of past subsidization. To the extent that a certain proportion of the residents of subsidized middle income housing would be forced, under privatization, to pay an excessive proportion of their income in rent, we might contemplate a limited, transitional period of rental subsidies. These subsidies would be dependent upon proof of income and paid for with some of the proceeds of the sale of the development.

In any case, there is no longer any excuse to believe that social engineers can succeed where private entrepreneurs have failed. New York's ownership of tax foreclosed housing has not improved housing conditions for city residents, yet it costs taxpayers hundreds of millions of dollars per year. Accordingly, New York City should get out of the slum housing business. This objective is not very difficult to achieve operationally, or even politically. The city's role as slum-lord-in-chief has not been especially popular with housing activists or tenants. In fact, as previously observed, the city stumbled into this role inadvertently when it shortened the tax delinquency grace period in the hopes of accelerating property tax payments during its mid-1970s fiscal crisis.

The sale of city-owned tax foreclosed housing to private owners would have several worthwhile results. The land sitting under the city's empty apartments would be freed up for new housing or other developments. The remaining occupied apartments would join the stock of low-cost private housing under conditions that we are certain would result in better maintenance and fairer allocation among potential tenants. Privatization and competition would insure a large and growing inventory of affordable private housing in New York City at a level of maintenance superior to any the city has been able or willing to provide. Apart from the benefits to the housing market that would attend the sale of the city's tax foreclosed housing, there would be a large fiscal windfall, too. The city would gain on three counts. It would realize the proceeds of the sale. It would be collecting property taxes from the new private owners. And perhaps most significantly, the city could devote its $248 million in Community Development Block Grant (CDBG) funds to more worthwhile community development projects.

The privatization of middle income and tax foreclosed public housing would still leave 166,000 apartments in the hands of the NYCHA. We are not proposing that these apartments be turned over to the private sector. There can be a legitimate role for publicly owned housing if it is not in competition with the private housing market. And by "private market," we mean privately owned, decent-quality housing offered at reasonable rents without subsidies. We recognize that there are a substantial number of households in New York City with incomes so low that they would not be able to afford even minimally decent apartments without some form of assistance. These and *only these* families should be eligible for apartments in the NYCHA inventory.

In other words, the role for publicly owned housing is to serve as a last resort, for the poorest families in the city. That is precisely the role envisioned for public housing under current federal government guidelines. The NYCHA, while increasingly sheltering the poorest families in New York, has assumed the role reluctantly. The reason for NYCHA's reluctance is that the poorest families are often the most troubled families. As such, they make life very difficult for the Housing Authority as operator and custodian of its housing developments, and they make life dangerous and unpleasant for their neighbors. It is therefore not surprising that the Housing Authority strains to recruit as tenants the most wholesome and often the most affluent of the households that would qualify under its and the federal government's income-eligibility guidelines.

Thus we are faced with a conundrum: if public housing serves lower middle income families because they are the best tenants, it competes with private housing unnecessarily and to the detriment of the efficient operation of New York City's housing market; if it serves only the poorest families, it risks, because of the behavior of a destructive minority of households, the accelerated deterioration of its housing facilities and undesirable social conditions for the majority of its tenants. We feel that there is a resolution to this dilemma, but it may require the cooperation of federal housing authorities and the courts. Public housing could serve the poorest families if high standards of tenant behavior could be enforced. The present controversy over the U.S. Department of Housing and Urban Development's (HUD) determination to evict the families of drug dealers points to the eventual adoption of more stringent behavioral standards for tenants in public housing. As it does in the private sector, destructive behavior would result in eviction. Present policy and court decisions make the eviction of destructive families by public housing agencies difficult, but this cannot justify offering a low-rent resource to families who should be living in privately owned apartments.

A Possible Dream

We have laid out an ambitious agenda of changes in New York City's and New York State's housing policies. Most of our proposals are highly controversial, and difficult to "sell" in the current political environment of the city and state. In proposing such "unrealistic" notions as rent deregulation and the sale of middle income housing, we feel justified on two counts.

First, we are convinced that fairly drastic measures must be contemplated to solve New York's housing problems. We also believe that the various subsidy and regulatory schemes proposed by public officials would hardly alleviate the situation and might make things worse.

Second, we are convinced that our proposals, if implemented, would transform housing conditions in New York City, and if implemented gradually, fairly, and competently would not impose hardships on any vulnerable families or individuals.

A Glimpse at the Deregulated Future

What would the housing market in New York City look like in the year 2005 if our various proposals were implemented? We are going to take a few of the indices of housing quality and market performance and compare New York's housing environment in 2005 with the state of affairs today. We have chosen this date for the comparison to allow enough time for the gradual adoption of our recommendations and for the new policies to have an impact on the city's housing market.

The estimates we make are predicated on the kind of drastic restructuring of New York's housing policies that we laid out earlier, one that replaces the present housing environment of excessive public regulation, ownership, and intervention with a housing market responsive to the forces of supply and demand, receptive both to the initiative of housing entrepreneurs and the needs and wishes of housing consumers. We are not prepared to dictate the precise form that these changes should take, or the many measures and adaptations that must necessarily accompany the transition from the present to the substantially freer housing arena that we envision. We merely wish to summarize the major features of the New York housing market that would have to be in place for our estimates to be valid:

1. Complete deregulation of rents throughout the rental housing market by the year 2000.

2. Revision of the zoning code, landmarking laws,environmental laws, and land-use review processes to allow extensive residential development in all presently designated nonresidential zones and permit higher residential densities in all areas other than the most intensively developed parts of Manhattan by 1995.

3. Liquidation by sale to entrepreneurs and tenants of the entire city-owned in rem inventory by 1995 and subsequent immediate resale of all future tax foreclosed properties.

4. Private ownership and market pricing of all Mitchell-Lama and other shallow-subsidy, publicly assisted housing developments by 1995, whether occurring naturally through expiration of statutory controls or through tenant or owner "buyouts."

5. Revision of the property tax system by 1995 such that assessment practices and rates would be uniform for all classes of residential property and all neighborhoods, keeping the effective property tax rate below 2.5 percent. This policy would include an end to pro-

grams of selective tax abatements for residential development or rehabilitation.

6. Substantial liberalization of co-op/condo conversion laws by
1995, allowing conversions to take place with fewer incumbent tenant purchases and the elimination of preferential standards for non-
eviction plans.

To the extent that only *some* of these policies are implemented, or
the time frame is extended, our estimates would have to be modified
accordingly.

By 2005 the most dramatic changes in the housing market would
be the ease with which an apartment or a house could be found, the
wide choice of dwellings available in size, location, and amenity, and
the reasonableness of rents and prices. It would be a housing market
with no windfall bargains, but neither would it have apartments or
homes that were outrageously priced, unless, of course, they were
outrageously luxurious, large, or particularly well located.

The external manifestation of these changes would be the wide-
spread evidence of new or recently completed construction and rehabilitation. The city would appear to be substantially rebuilt and
revitalized, especially in those areas of the outer boroughs that have
been the most deteriorated or neglected.

The engine of all these changes would be an increasingly rapid
pace of new residential development, first becoming significant
around 1993 and approaching post-World War II housing production peaks around 2005. The rising rates of housing production—resulting from anticipated deregulation policies—would permit the retirement of the city's oldest and worst housing even as it replenishes
the housing stock sufficiently to produce a growing vacancy rate in
the rental and ownership markets. Rising rates of housing production would also accommodate a modest growth in the city's population.

There is no question that one of the fundamental changes accom-
panying deregulation and new development would be a housing
price structure that would make housing somewhat more expensive
for most New York households and a great deal more expensive in
particular market niches. This is not an unfortunate by-product of
the changes we anticipate, but an absolutely necessary facilitator of
these changes. Most of the problems of New York's present housing

market, including the egregious misallocation of the existing stock and the anemic pace of unsubsidized new construction and rehabilitation, result from constraints on housing prices. Housing prices must rise, to reallocate older housing properly and to call forth new development.

The overall effect of the new price structure would be a more equitable distribution of housing burdens. The poorest New Yorkers are expected to experience *lower* rent-income ratios, while those in the highest income deciles would experience considerably *higher* rent-income ratios, but these would be commensurate with increases in quality. Because the transition to this world of rational housing prices would be gradual, there would be very few if any households who would experience a wrenching increase in rent. The housing environment in 2005 would simply not encompass as many great bargains as the housing market of 1990. The most dramatic changes in housing prices would be seen in the better neighborhoods of Manhattan. Even here, however, the rents of vacant apartments may well be lower (in inflation-adjusted terms) than they are today even as the average rents rise considerably. But regardless of the specific magnitudes involved, the direction of change resulting from our recommendations would eliminate the most common injustices of the existing scarcity by design.

APPENDIX A

Lease Succession and Tenure Rights

Tenure is the right to remain in one's apartment and renew a lease. In an unregulated market, the expiration of a lease permits both landlords and tenants to renegotiate terms. And in the absence of a new agreement, the landlord would be free not to renew the lease and to force the tenant to move.

Any politically effective form of rent regulation, by contrast, will have tenure rules that are generous to tenants, so that they will support the politicians who are granting the regulatory benefits. According to New York's rent regulation program, tenants have "statutory" leases, meaning that they can stay forever if they wish without a signed lease. In rent stabilization, tenants are eligible for an endless succession of automatic lease renewals, which amounts to the same thing.

One might expect that even under tenant-favoring tenure rules, landlords might regain possession of their apartments in the event of blatant lease violations such as non-payment of rent, or when a tenant moves or dies. In New York, this is not the case. While non-payment of rent or damage to premises are grounds for lease-termination in most cities around the country, New York City's courts will often rule in favor of the tenants if partial rent payments are made or if the building has some outstanding code violations. Under this system, primary tenants have near-total security, while roommates, and those who share or sublet existing apartments, have no security at all.

Consider the stories of two sublet tenants.

Linda Schwartz, a thirty-two-year-old teacher, has been sharing a large Upper West Side apartment with four other people and has been looking for a new apartment for the last few weeks.

"I don't really know if the apartments I'm looking at are rent-controlled or not, because I'm looking at shares and sublets," she says. "The individuals with the leases are doing what they want. Some are offering fair deals, some aren't."

"What I feel is that people are paying a reasonable amount but charging a lot more. I could be wrong, but I feel like people are paying $600 for an apartment and charging me $500 to be a roommate. It's fair and it's not fair. It bothers me a little bit that everybody's getting into it and overcharging." (Interview conducted in summer of 1985.)

As Linda suggests, primary tenants (those with the lease) can rent out extra apartment space at whatever rate the market will fetch; the choice to rent it out is theirs. The primary tenant can rent to the highest bidder, or he can offer a bargain rent to a lover or a friend. He can even do a little bit of both, making money and friends, for there is no one more desirable in New York than someone with a stabilized apartment.

Jenny Jozwiak, a twenty-three-year-old photographer, is losing her low-rent apartment share in the Columbia University area. Her situation shows how having connections is crucial to getting a cheap apartment.

"The apartment is actually rented by a friend of my roommate's mom, and she's subletting to us," Jenny explains, "But my roommate's living with her boyfriend now, and it's a bit more her apartment than mine."

Jenny's rent is skyrocketing from her present $141.50 for a share to something in the $375 range. She has already found shares for this amount in Park Slope, Brooklyn, and on West 101st Street in Manhattan, in neighborhoods that she terms "funky."

"I've been lucky ever since I've been in Manhattan. I've never had to pay more than $160 a month rent. I've always been really lucky, but now my luck's run out. I'll have to pay what everyone else has been paying. It's hard to get used to that." (Interview conducted in summer of 1985.)

Jenny's friend got to keep the low-rent apartment because of a lucky family friendship and an abuse of the housing-tenure rules on the part of the friend. While the subletting rules require the primary tenant to remain in occupancy, many tenants evade these rules by renting mailboxes, registering telephones in different names, returning to the apartment on occasion, or other ruses. Since enforcement is left to the landlord, who often has only a small incentive (the 15 percent vacancy allowance), many of these evasion strategies are successful.

The extent of the sublet market shows the degree to which property rights, wealth, and income have been transferred from landlords and prospective residents to primary tenants. The landlord receives a below-market rent from the primary tenant because of rent regulation. The sublet tenant pays an above-normal rent to the primary tenant because of the shortage created by rent regulation. The only winner from this process is the primary tenant, who not only pays a below-market rent for his housing but also receives a monthly side payment for his incumbency.

Nevertheless, since the subletting rules still require the primary tenant to live in the apartment, a lease is not a completely transferable property right like an ownership title, and the primary tenant is unable to capture the full value of his leasehold. Ideally, the tenant might prefer to move out of the regulated apartment entirely, rent the space, and use the proceeds to rent or purchase a preferred apartment. Under New York law, however, when a primary tenant moves out and lives in another apartment, he relinquishes his status and becomes vulnerable to eviction for "nonprimary residence." If a tenant wishes to sublet his entire apartment for any length of time, he must notify the landlord and charge no more than 10 percent above his primary rent, regardless of how much below market the primary rent is. We suspect that the prohibition against subletting apartments at market rates will never be repealed, partly because it would undermine the legal basis for rent control and partly because rent regulation is seen by most voters as a reward for active renters, not for absentee ones.

In the meantime, the incentive for primary tenants and subletters to break this rule is extremely powerful, and because of the practice, the courts are constantly arbitrating residence cases. However, the costs of *proving* cases of illegal subletting are considerable, and under rent stabilization, the only benefit to the owner from such a lawsuit is a chance to select a new tenant and a 15 percent rent increase. The only circumstances where enforcing this law is profitable is with a regulated tenant or in a converted building, where the full-market versus regulated gap is at stake.

Still, the *degree* to which subletting and absentee tenants are distorting the rent regulatory system is unknown. The Census's Housing and Vacancy Survey does not ask whether the current household or part of the household is subletting from another tenant and what the terms of the transaction might be. Of course, such a question would have to be carefully asked in order to insure the confidentiality and accuracy of the response, but the information would certainly be valuable. With the data that is currently collected, sublet tenants of regulated primary tenants have remained uncounted and ignored.

Succession Rights

What happens when the present tenant leaves? Who gets the vacant apartment? Consider the case of Michael Brown and Robert Hayes, gay lovers who shared a rent-stabilized apartment on West Twenty-second Street in Manhattan. Hayes contracted AIDS and after a long illness died in January 1985. Hayes, however, was the only tenant named on the lease. When he died, the landlord, Two Associates, sought to evict Brown on the grounds that he was not the tenant of record (*Real Estate Weekly*, April 27, 1987 and January 25, 1988; *City Limits*, February, 1988).

In an unregulated market, succession rights are never an issue. Upon a death in a family or household, a wise landlord will extend the present lease to the tenant's survivors and avoid having the apartment unrented. If an uncaring landlord demands a rent increase from a tenant's widow, surviving children, or ex-roommate, they can usually find a comparable apartment at a more reasonable rent. In New York's regulated market, however, the complicated legal question of who is entitled to occupy the city's cheap vacant apartments has grown to explosive proportions. Consequently, the succession issue has become entangled with other debates concerning common-law marriages, gay rights, divorce settlements, custody battles, and adoption rules that accompany today's varying family patterns.

For many years, the law on succession in New York seemed quite clear. Spouses and children of the tenant on the lease could continue to live in the apartment should the tenant die or get divorced, provided that they had lived in the apartment since the inception of the relationship. Over time, lower New York State courts came to recognize succession rights for the surviving member of a gay relationship. However, the law did not recognize any succession rights for roommates, sublet tenants, or live-in lovers.

The 1983 renewal of the Emergency Tenant Protection Act made it easier for landlords to bring eviction cases before the courts, and several recent cases before the State Court of Appeals challenged the status quo. In the case of *Sullivan* v. *Brevard Associates*, the Appellate Division ruled that landlords were not required to issue a renewal lease to family members should the tenant on the lease die or move out (Metz 1988).

The State Department of Housing and Community Renewal (DHCR) responded to the Sullivan ruling by issuing Emergency Bulletin 85–1, to clarify state law and list those family members who should be issued renewal leases upon a vacancy. This bulletin attempted to broaden the traditional court definition of family members by including nephews, nieces, and in-laws, and offered more limited renewal rights to non-family residents.

When the case of *Two Associates* v. *Michael Brown* was decided, the State Appellate Division ruled the DHCR administrative bulletin to be invalid. While the County Supreme Court found Brown to be a family member under the DHCR bulletin, the State Appellate Division ruled that the DHCR acted beyond its authority and that Brown was not entitled to the apartment.

The current legal status of lease succession is murky, with some courts ruling in favor of landlords and some in favor of tenants. As long as a lease is not a voluntary contract between two parties but a one-sided legal obligation, the issue of succession rights will remain contentious. In effect, these extended tenure rights represent a partial transfer of the ownership of the apartment from the landlord to the tenant and are accordingly capitalized in a further diminution of its market value.

APPENDIX B

Notes on the History of Rent Regulation

Creation of the Maximum Base Rent System

At the same time that rent stabilization was being imposed on post-war apartments, the city recognized that low rent levels in prewar, rent-controlled apartments were leading to declining quality levels and housing abandonment. Just before Mayor Lindsay's re-election in November 1969, Housing Administrator Jason Nathan told the press that he backed the need for rent increases for rent-controlled apartments (*New York Times*, November 8, 1969. See also *New York Times*, December 12, 1969). Nathan cited figures from a forthcoming city-sponsored study by the New York City Rand Institute about the effects of rent control on the city's growing housing abandonment problem. In early leaks to the press, the Rand study purportedly claimed that rent controls kept rents below the $20–25 per room needed for adequate maintenance and reasonable profit. Subsequent to making these remarks, however, Nathan resigned his housing post, reportedly forced out by Reform Democrats who were alarmed at his comments on rent control.

In December, however, the city's criticism of rent control continued. The mayor's Rent Control Committee, headed by New York University Law School Dean Robert McKay, recommended major changes in the rent-control program, including a guaranteed minimum rent per room and low income tenant rent subsidies, distributed directly or through tax abatements to owners (Keating, 1978). Despite pressure from the press, Albert A. Walsh, Nathan's replacement, refused to make the complete Rand study public and denied the reported finding that rent control was the leading contributor to the abandonment problem. Walsh argued, "I'm sure rent control is a factor, but it's not the only factor by any means: the climate of a particular neighborhood, the impact of crime, narcotics" (*New York Times*, January 7, 1970). Walsh said he considered the housing decay problem a national phenomenon and a far more complicated process than the Rand study indicated. For his part, Mayor Lindsay was believed to stand firmly against any relaxation of rent control.

On February 5, ten city councilmen got the State Supreme Court to direct Walsh to indicate why the Rand study should not be made public (*New York Times*, February 6, 1970). Councilman Leon Katz called the report essential for the city to review its rent-control legislation.

One week later, additional portions of the Rand study were leaked to the press. The study found that the average rent for a rent-controlled apartment was $54 per month below the market level which, for 1.2 million apartments, amounted to a $807 million annual income transfer from landlords to tenants ($45 per family per month × 12 month, × 1.2 million families, equals $807 million per year. *New York Times*, February 13, 1970). The study advised that a relaxation of the city's rent-control law must be linked to a $130 million a year city program of rent subsidies to needy families. The report called the city's rent-control program a short-sighted attempt to protect renters from the effects of a housing shortage and rising costs.

The study also found that while rents had been allowed to rise only 2 percent per year since 1945 in rent-controlled buildings, maintenance costs had risen 6 percent, taxes had risen between 4 to 6 percent, and interest rates had doubled.

In response to these reports, Administrator Walsh and Commissioner of Rent and Housing Maintenance Benjamin Altman indicated that they would support the relaxation of rent controls under a plan that would tie rent increases to capital improvements and maintenance (*New York Times*, February 15, 1970). While criticizing some of the Rand Study's methods, they favored the study's idea of public subsidies to low income tenants to help pay for the increased rents.

On April 30, a second city-sponsored study of rent control was released, continuing the pressure on the mayor to reform the regulations. Professor George Sternlieb of Rutgers University released his report, "The Urban Housing Dilemma," which claimed that over half of all rent-controlled buildings were failing to make economic profits (*New York Times*, May 1, 1970). Although he considered higher rents to be a necessary condition for ending the multiplying quantity of decayed and abandoned apartments, Sternlieb attributed part of the housing problem to landlords' failure to collect the maximum legal rent either because of incompetence or a racist desire to keep white tenants from leaving their building. While not recommending a specific "minimum rent" formula for rent-controlled apartments, the Sternlieb report echoed landlords' calls for reform of rent control.

On May 12 Mayor Lindsay finally proposed a radical, comprehensive reform of the rent-control laws, closely following the Rand and Sternlieb findings (*New York Times*, May 13, 1970). Lindsay's plan called for a 10 percent rent increase for all rent-controlled apartments on July 1 and for additional increases thereafter. Moreover, the proposed measure would take the responsibility of setting rents away from the city council and give it instead to the city's Rent and Housing Maintenance Department. The department would compute a target rent, known as the Maximum Base Rent, for every rent-controlled apartment in the city. The Maximum Base Rent (MBR) was to be an "economic rent," based on estimates of the landlords' operating and financing costs, and including a provision for the owner's profit. Mayor Lindsay implicitly recognized the responsibility of rent control for causing housing deterioration. The mayor declared, "The housing crisis requires this kind of thorough reorganization and modernization if we are to reverse the tide of housing deterioration and free housing from the inequities and antagonisms of the past."

On June 27, 1970, the city council approved Lindsay's MBR program by a vote of 27 to 10, and the mayor signed the bill on July 10th (*New York Times*, June 28, 1970 and July 11, 1970). Under the MBR program, the landlord was permitted to increase the tenant's rent by 15 percent every two years until the rent reached the MBR target. Rents for vacated units were permitted to rise to the full MBR. As the MBR was a moving target that was adjusted as costs rose, the MBR level would only be a binding constraint following a change in tenancy. Nevertheless, the MBR reform meant that a rent-controlled apartment building's rents would begin to approach the building's costs.

Vacancy Decontrol

This plan, put forth by Governor Rockefeller, was seen as administratively simple, important for the economic health of rent-controlled buildings, crucial for attracting investment from financial institutions, and not adverse to existing tenants, who would be protected by rent control and anti-eviction laws.

Rockefeller's vacancy decontrol proposal was strongly criticized by the Lindsay administration, which argued that the anti-eviction laws would not be able to stop concerted landlord harassment (*New York Times*, April 29, 1971). Urstadt and Kristof, the principal architects of vacancy decontrol, disputed this claim (*New York Times*, May 6, 1971).

The Vacancy Decontrol Law passed the state legislature on May 26, 1971, by a narrow margin (*New York Times*, May 27, 1971). With turnover of apartments continuing at rates of 10–15%, a growing portion of the rental stock would be decontrolled and in a period of ten to twenty years, rent regulations would gradually wither away.

In retrospect, the MBR system and vacancy decontrol brought enormous changes in the financial well-being of the city's apartment buildings (and their owners). Between July 1971 and December 1973, an estimated 250,000 to 300,000 rent-controlled apartments were decontrolled, and an estimated 88,000 rent-stabilized apartments were "destabilized," or taken out of the rent-control program. In his analysis of the period, Frank Kristof found that $445 million of the $807 million "rent gap" that the 1968 Rand study identified had been closed by 1973 by the MBR system and the vacancy decontrol law. Kristof attributed most of the $445 million closing to the new MBR system. Specifically, $277 million was achieved by MBR increases in apartments that did not have a vacancy between 1971–73. Of the $168 million gap closed in the 250–300,000 apartments that did have a vacancy, Kristof estimated that $95 million would have achieved under the MBR system, even if there was no vacancy. Only $73 million in additional income to building owners was directly attributable to vacancy decontrol (Kristof, 1974).

Put in terms of average rent levels, between 1968 and 1971 the mean rent in controlled apartments rose from $85 to $110, again mostly attributable to MBR. Apartments that had a vacancy in the 1971–73 period rose from a mean rent of $110 to $155 after the vacancy decontrol, finally rising to a 1973 level of $160, the new market rent level. Mean rents in apartments that did not have a vacancy rose from $110 to $137 between 1971–73, an increase again fully attributable to the MBR program (Kristof, 1974). This $23 rent gap between the $160 market rent and the $137 controlled rent was less than half the $54 per apartment gap found in the 1968 Rand study.

Factors Contributing to the End of Vacancy Decontrol

First, the accelerating rate of inflation in the early 1970s made the rent increases resulting from vacancy decontrol even higher than anticipated. Not only were rents rising from regulated levels to market levels, but rising also to cover expected future inflation. President Nixon's announcement on August 15, 1971, of a program of wage and price controls made Rockefeller's decontrol experiment and the MBR program appear counterproductive, perhaps even unpatriotic. Vacancy decontrol was halted during Nixon's 90-day freeze, and Mayor Lindsay stopped all MBR increases (*New York Times*, August 17, 1971 and October 8, 1971). After several months of disputes over whether local rent-control programs should be exempt from Federal controls, New York City's rent-controlled and rent-stabilized apartments were removed from Nixon's so-called Phase II price control program. Vacated apartments that were decontrolled by the Vacancy Decontrol Law were subsequently governed by Phase II, but these controls permitted regular increases and generous capital improvement allowances (Keating, 1978). The chief impact of federal price controls was political, not economic.

The end of federal price controls on January 11, 1973, came amidst a growing clamor of tenant protests about rising rents. Unlike the end of price controls after World War II, monetary policy in the 1970s remained loose so that rising demand kept rents and prices rising. Tenant organizations led a number of protests against MBR rent increases in 1972, and several prominent tenant leaders (Jesse Gray, Frank Barbaro, and John Dearie) won election to the State Assembly in 1972 and 1973. Again in response to the "inflation problem," Assemblyman Andrew Stein used his chairmanship of the Temporary State Commission on Living Costs and the Economy as a forum to criticize the effects of vacancy decontrol.

The second intervening event was the pending expiration of the Rent Stabilization Law in 1974. The city council voted unanimously on March 21, 1974, to extend the law for another five years (*New York Times*, March 22, 1974). Attention shifted to Albany, where, following this initial victory, tenant leaders were firm in their commitment to end vacancy decontrol.

The Extension of Rent Regulation

Governor Wilson's original ETPA proposal would have ended vacancy decontrol by granting new tenants the right to challenge their new rent level before a new Rent Regulation Authority. The city's Rent Guidelines Board would be abolished in favor of a new Rent Standards Board, which would also issue city-wide guidelines. Rent-controlled apartments would remain under the MBR system except for certain "luxury" apartments—those renting for more than $500 per month. Finally and perhaps most important, Wilson's ETPA extended rent regulation to areas outside New York City with a rental vacancy rate below 6 percent (Keating, 1978). Here, Wilson was clearly aiming to win votes in the New York suburbs in his fall election campaign.

As a bill that offered something to many constituencies, Wilson's proposal left no one completely pleased. Nevertheless, extension of rent regulation into the suburbs meant that support for the package crossed party and ideological lines and forced Republican legislative leaders to devise an alternative or else lose control of the legislative initiative.

Over one-half million apartments were put into the rent stabilization program by ETPA, more than doubling the coverage of the program. The ETPA reimposed rent stabilization for most of the apartments that had been removed from rent control and rent stabilization in the 1971–74 period and placed control on all apartments constructed since 1969, approximately 110,000 previously destabilized apartments, 400,000 decontrolled apartments, and 7,500 newly built apartments (Keating, 1978).

Not only had the workload of the Rent Stabilization Association and the Conciliation and Appeals Board been greatly increased by the ETPA, but the power of the Rent Guidelines Board had been greatly enhanced, too. All units in "large" buildings became destined for rent stabilization under ETPA. If the unit was presently in stabilization, it would remain so. If the unit had become decontrolled, subsequent rents could only increase by the Rent Guidelines Board's schedule. If the unit was in the rent-control program, it would experience a one-time decontrol upon vacancy. Once the landlord and tenant had negotiated a new "fair market rent," that rent became stabilized and governed by the future increase limits set by the Rent Guidelines Board.

This "fair market rent" itself became politicized as tenants were given a 60-day period in which to challenge whether the agreed-upon rent figure exceeded prevailing levels. Tenant activists quickly alerted potential renters to immediately challenge their initially agreed-upon rents to test whether it met the "fair market" test.

Apartments in small buildings (those with fewer than six units) were treated much more gently, presumably out of a feeling of support for small landlords. All units in small buildings were scheduled to be decontrolled upon vacancy, just as the previous law had allowed. Decontrolled units remained decontrolled; controlled units were decontrolled upon the next vacancy.

Finally and most importantly, any unit that reached the stabilization program would have its rent capped indefinitely. Landlords were permitted only an additional 15% rent increase, known today as the "vacancy allowance," for any lease following a vacancy, known as a "vacancy lease." The vacancy allowance feature meant that landlords had lost an important escape valve that would justify their operation of a rental buildings even when current rents were below cost. The rent that the landlord and his first tenant agreed to initially would not only govern their agreement for the next year and the year after but would constrain his income for generations to come.

APPENDIX C

Homeless Housing

Homeless individuals have lived in New York for many years; known at different times as hobos, tramps, transients, or bums, they have been treated to diverse city policies, ranging from the jailing of alcoholics and vagrants to the sheltering or institutionalizing of the homeless (Blau, 1987). In the last ten years homelessness has become an explosive public issue, at times overshadowing all other issues related to housing.

Contrary to popular rhetoric, however, homelessness is *not* primarily a housing issue, but rather a complex social phenomenon resulting from adverse conditions of mental and physical disability, substance abuse, and social isolation. The lack of a home is merely a common denominator among a disparate group of troubled individuals who have shown up at the city's doorstep. As Tom Bethell has noted:

> Groups that are defined by the absence of a characteristic are very confusing and are not real groups. And "homeless" is one of these groups. "The homeless" is a group defined by the absence of a characteristic. This is confusing because it imputes a kind of false homogeneity to a large number of people, who may not have very much in common, except that they lack something, namely a home . . . Entirely diverse groups are lumped together under the false unifying label of homeless: deinstitutionalized mental patients, drug addicts, and substance abusers in general, and some bona fide unemployed people. (Bethell, 1988)

This confusion about the nature of homelessness has led to a set of conflicting policies and programs, on the part of both the city and federal governments and the homeless advocates themselves. In the 1980s, the federal government saw homelessness as a short-term crisis caused by the economic downturn, and responded by redirecting disaster-relief funds and allowing the diversion of Community Development Block Grants to house the homeless. With the passage of the McKinney Homeless Assistance Act of 1987, some sixteen separate programs were developed to address homelessness under the Departments of Housing and Urban Development, Agriculture, Education, Health and Human Services, Labor, the Federal Emergency Management Agency, and the General Services Administration. Despite all of these efforts, however, the job of responding to homelessness and the management of services to them would always require local initiative. The federal government has merely sought to fund the efforts of local governments by establishing a number of aid programs; New York City is simply among the most proficient users in applying them.

The advocates' strategy has centered on using state courts to force New York City to provide services for the homeless that the municipal legislature and city council would not permit. In 1979, attorney Robert Hayes filed a class-action suit against the city, known as the Callaghan case, on behalf of three homeless men claiming a right-to-shelter existing under the state constitution.

Hayes won a preliminary injunction from the State Supreme Court, and the city opened the Keener Building, a closed state psychiatric hospital on Ward's Island, to house homeless men. The next year, Hayes filed suit again, claiming insufficient staffing and a lack of medical, psychiatric, and other services. As the Callaghan case went to trial, the city and state avoided the risk of losing in court and signed a consent degree with Hayes to "Provide shelter and board to each homeless man who applies for it; provided that: (a) the man meets the need standard for the homeless relief program established in New York State; or (b) the man by reason of physical, mental, or social dysfunction is in need of temporary shelter" (cited at Blau, 1987, p. 126). From the Callaghan case onward, the city's population of homeless men (and more recently, homeless families) arriving at city shelters began to escalate rapidly. This growth in the sheltered population can lead to several possible hypotheses. One is that the number of homeless in the city is growing rapidly, owing to economic conditions, drug abuse, or deinstitutionalization of the mentally ill. Two, the number of homeless in the city is stable, but more of the homeless are leaving the streets and taking the city's offer of a roof, a bed, and a warm meal. Three, the city's homeless population may or may not be growing, but the unconditional offer of free shelter is attracting much of the city's marginally housed population.

However, the evidence for judging the validity of these various propositions is meager. All research on the homeless is dogged by three problems: defining the homeless, counting them, and finding a representative sample to describe and analyze. The definition and counting problems include whether to count shelter and/or street populations; whether to count and describe the homeless as individuals or by the family unit; whether to count residents of battered women's shelters, alcohol-detoxification centers, jails, and other institutions; and whether to include individuals or families living "doubled up" in the apartments of other individuals or families. Since one study may choose to include one group and not another, comparing the results of any two studies is problematic. The definition of homelessness, moreover, can be expanded or contracted in order to dramatize or understate the problem. We must recognize that no scientific count exists of the number of street homeless in New York.[1]

The most important question, of course, is whether the primary problem for the homeless is merely housing. While the difficulties of counting the street homeless make accurate judgments about their characteristics and needs impossible, we can look at a number of studies of the shelter homeless population. These studies show that perhaps half of the homeless suffer from one or more forms of substance abuse. At least one third are mentally ill and have had prior mental hospitalization. And a majority of the single men have spent time in jail or prison (Rossi, 1989).

Therefore, the homeless should not be thought of merely as a sector of the poor who could not find housing. America's and New York's homeless populations suffer from a multiplicity of social problems beyond the lack of shelter. Those suffering from severe physical and mental disabilities would have problems finding housing in any market. Those with drug abuse problems and prison histories may be isolated from their families and friends and will have great difficulty reintegrating into society. Finally, large numbers of single mothers with children seek shelter in New York. Given the long waiting lists for public housing, homeless families may be looking for a way of jumping the queue to publicly provided housing. The lesson is that we must be careful not to let our efforts to help the mentally ill and substance abusers drive and distort the city's housing policy.

Works Cited

Arthur D. Little, Inc. May 5, 1986. *A Tale of Two Cities: Rent Regulation in New York City—Does All New York Benefit Equally?* Cambridge, Mass.: Arthur D. Little, Inc.

————1987. *Housing Gridlock in New York.* Cambridge, Mass.: Arthur D. Little, Inc.

Barnett, Jonathan. 1982. *An Introduction to Urban Design.* New York: Harper and Row.

Barreto, Felix Ramon. May 1986. "The Effects of Rent Control on Housing Production, Valuation, and Tax Shifts." Ph.D. diss., New Brunswick: Rutgers University.

Berenyi, Eileen Brettler. 1989. "Locally Funded Housing Programs in the United States: A Survey of the 51 Most Populated Cities." New York: New School for Social Research, Community Development Research Center.

Bethell, Tom. December 14, 1988. "Rethinking Policy on Homelessness." Heritage Lectures No. 194 (transcript). Washington, D.C.: Heritage Foundation.

Blau, Joel S. "The Homeless of New York: A Case Study in Social Welfare Policy." Ph.D. diss., New York: Columbia University School of Social Work.

Block, Walter. 1972. "The Economics of Rent Control in the United States." Ph.D. diss., New York: Columbia University.

Brookes, Warren J. July 15, 1986. "Proposition 2 1/2: Massachusetts' Dirty Little Secret." *Wall Street Journal.*

Citizens Budget Commission. December 1987. "New York City's Housing Crisis: What Has Government Spent?" New York: Citizens Budget Commission.

Citizens Housing Council of New York. September 1947. *CHC Housing News* 6:1.

Crespo, Marcos A. November 30, 1986. Letter to John Gilbert III. New York: Rent Stabilization Association files.

Czander, William. May 22, 1987. Sworn testimony quoted in "Renew Legislation of Housing—Letter of Support," Kepasi Realty Co., 313 W. 100 St. New York: Rent Stabilization Association Files.

DeSalvo, Joseph S. 1971. *Reforming Rent Control in New York City: Analysis of Housing Expenditures and Market Rentals.* Santa Monica: The Rand Corporation.

Downs, Anthony. 1988. *Residential Rent Controls: An Evaluation.* Washington, D.C.: Urban Land Institute.

Epstein, Richard A. 1985. *Takings: Private Property and the Power of Eminent Domain.* Cambridge, Mass.: Harvard University Press.

Freeman, Richard B. and Brian Hall. September, 1986. "Permanent Homelessness in America?" National Bureau of Economic Research Working Paper No. 2013. Washington, D.C.: National Bureau of Economic Research.

Hamilton, Rabinovitz, Szanton, and Alschuler, Inc., and the Urban Institute. April 1985. "Rental Housing Study: The Rent Stabilization System—Impacts and Alternatives." Los Angeles: City of Los Angeles Rent Stabilization Division.

Howe, Edward and Donald Reeb. 1985. "The Political Economy of the Property Tax." In *New York State Today,* ed. Peter W. Colby. Albany, N.Y.: SUNY Press.

Keating, William D. 1978. "Landlord Self-Regulation: New York City's Rent Stabilization System 1968–1978." Ph.d. diss., Berkeley: University of California.

Kingsbridge Heights Neighborhood Improvement Association. April 17, 1986. Transcript of meeting. New York: Rent Stabilization Association files.

Kristof, Frank. January 28, 1974. "Vacancy Decontrol in New York City." Unpublished paper prepared for the New York State Urban Development Corporation.

————1975. Economic Facets of New York City's Problems. In *Agenda for a City,* ed. Lyle C. Fitch and Anne Marie H. Walsh. New York: Institute of Public Administration.

Lee, Barrett A. May 2, 1989. "Stability and Change in an Urban Homeless Population." *Demography* 26:2.

Lett, Monica. 1976. *Rent Control: Concepts, Realities, and Mechanisms.* New Brunswick: Center for Urban Policy Research of Rutgers University.

Los Angeles Community Development Department. 1987. "Rental Housing Study: Executive Summary Prepared For the City of Los Angeles." Los Angeles: Community Development Department.

Lowry, Ira S. April 1985. "The Financial Performance of Rental Property under Rent Control: Berkeley, California, 1978–1985." Santa Monica: California Housing Research Institute.

Marcuse, Peter. January 1977. "Rental Housing in the City of New York." New York: City of New York.

Metz, Jeffrey. January 25, 1988. "New Rent Code Raises Issues Regarding Succession." *Real Estate Weekly.*

Moorehouse, John C. July 1972. Optimal Housing Maintenance Under Rent Control. *Southern Economic Journal* 39:93–106.

New York City Comptroller, 1986. "Annual Financial Report of the Comptroller for the Fiscal Year Ended June 30, 1986." New York: New York City Comptroller, 1986.

New York City Department of City Planning. 1984. "New Housing in New York City 1984." New York: New York City Department of City Planning.

——1986. New York City Department of City Planning, New Housing in New York City 1986. New York: New York City Department of City Planning.

New York City Housing Development Administration and Department of Consumer Affairs. February 8, 1969. "Report to the Mayor on an Investigation into Rental Increases in the Non-Controlled Housing Market." New York: New York City Housing Development Administration and Department of Consumer Affairs.

New York City Rent Guidelines Board. 1969. "Report of the Rent Guidelines Board to Mayor Lindsay." New York: New York City Rent Guidelines Board.

New York City Office of Management and Budget. "Message of the the Mayor, Fiscal Year 1987." New York: New York City Office of Management and Budget.

"New York City, Office of the Mayor. February 15, 1989. "Mayor's Management Report." New York: New York City, Office of the Mayor.

New York State Board of Equalization and Assessment. 1983. "Taxation at the Constitutional Limit: A Status Report on Real Property Taxes in New York State, 1975–1982."

New York State Department of Housing and Community Renewal, Office of Rent Administration. January 1987. "Restructuring the Rent Regulatory System: A Report to the Governor." Albany: New York State, Department of Housing and Community Renewal, Office of Rent Administration.

New York State Department of Social Services. October 1984. "Homelessness in New York State: A Report to the Governor and the Legislature." Vol. 1. Albany: New York State Department of Social Services.

New York State Reconstruction Commission. March 1920. "Housing Conditions, Report of the Housing Committee of the Reconstruction Commission of the State of New York." New York: New York State Reconstruction Commission.

New York State Tenant and Neighborhood Coalition. August 1988.
"NYSTNC Fact Sheet." New York: New York State Tenant and Neighborhood Coalition.

Olson, Edgar O. November-December 1972. An Econometric Model of Rent
Control. *Journal of Political Economy* 80(6):1081–1100.

———1981. "Questions and Some Answers about Rent Control: An Empir-
ical Analysis of New York's Experience." In *Rent Control: Myths and Realities*, ed. Walter Block and Edgar Olsen. Vancouver: The Fraser Institute.

Penn Central Transportation Company v. City of New York, 438 U.S. at 129 and
at 141.

Peterson, George E., Arthur B. Solomon, William C. Apgar, Jr., and Hadi
Madjid. 1973. *Property Taxes, Housing and the Cities*. New York: D.C.
Heath.

Rex Management Corporation. January 1, 1986. Letter to Frank Ricci/Rent
Stabilization Association. New York: Rent Stabilization Association files.

Rose, Joseph B. 1985. "Landmarks Preservation: Considering the Costs."
New York Affairs 8:4:146.

Rydell, Peter, and Kevin Neets. 1985. "Direct Effects of Undermaintenance
and Deterioration." In *The Rent Control Debate*, ed. Paul L. Niebanck.
Chapel Hill: University of North Carolina Press.

Rydell, C. Peter, et al. August 1981. *The Impact of Rent Control on the Los Angeles Housing Market*. Santa Monica: The Rand Corporation.

Salins, Peter. 1980. *The Ecology of Housing Destruction*. New York: New York
University Press.

Settlement Housing Fund, Inc. 1987. "Evaluation of Housing New York:
Final Report to the Robert Sterling Clark Foundation and the Taconic
Foundation." New York: Settlement Housing Fund, Inc.

Schwartz, Joel. 1989. "Tenant Power in the Liberal City, 1943–71." In *The
Tenant Movement in New York City, 1904–84*, ed. Ronald Lawson. New
Brunswick, N.J.: Rutgers University Press.

Stegman, Michael A. 1982. "The Dynamics of Rental Housing in New York
City." New York: Department of Housing Preservation and Development.

———1985. "Housing in New York: Study of a City, 1984." New York: Department of Housing Preservation and Development.

———1985. "The Model: Rent Control in New York City." In *The Rent Control Debate*, ed. Paul L. Niebanck. Chapel Hill: The University of North
Carolina Press.

————1988. "Housing and Vacancy Report: New York City, 1987." New York: Department of Housing Preservation and Development.

Sternlieb, George, Monica Lett, and others. 1975. *Rent Control in Fort Lee, New Jersey.* New Brunswick, N.J.: Rutgers University, Center for Urban Policy Research.

Sternlieb, George, and Robert W. Lake. September 1976. "Dynamics of Real Estate Tax Delinquency." *National Tax Journal* 29(3):261–271.

Swan, Herbert S. 1944. *The Housing Market in New York City.* New York: Reinhold.

Tobier, Emmanuel, and Elizabeth Roistacher. 1986. "Housing Policy." In *Setting Municipal Priorities: American Cities and the New York Experience,* ed. Raymond Horton and Charles Brecher. New York: New York University Press.

Tobier, Emmanuel, and Barbara Gordon Espejo. 1988. "Housing. In *The Two New York's: State-City Relations in the Changing Federal System,* ed. Gerald Benjamin and Charles Brecher. New York: Sage Publications.

Trilogical Enterprises, Inc. Undated memo. New York: Rent Stabilization Association files.

United States Bureau of the Census. 1980. *Census of Housing.* Washington, D.C.: Goverment Printing Office.

United States Bureau of Labor Statistics. 1984. Monthly Labor Review, January 1984.

United States Congress. 1953. *Congressional Quarterly Annual Report 1953.* Washington, D.C.: Government Printing Office.

————1981–86. "Housing Units Authorized by Building Permits." Washington, D.C.: Goverment Printing Office.

United States Department of Commerce. 1985. *American Housing Survey for the United States in 1985.* Washington D.C.: Government Printing Office.

United States Department of Housing and Urban Development. May 1984. "A Report to the Secretary on the Homeless and Emergency Shelters." Washington, D.C.: Government Printing Office.

————September 1991. "Report to Congress on Rent Control." Washington, D.C.: Government Printing Office.

United States Department of Housing and Urban Development and U.S. Bureau of the Census. 1987. *Annual Housing Survey.* Washington, D.C.: Government Printing Office.

White, Michelle J. 1986. Property Taxes and Housing Abandonment. *Journal of Urban Economics* 20(3):312–330.

Winthrop Gardens, et al. v. Eimicke. 58 AD. 2d 764, 396NYS 2d 400, 1977. Sworn affidavit submitted in support of petitioners. 1977.

Zabarkes, Arthur. 1980. "Zoning Continued: Get Me Rewrite." *New York Affairs* 6:3:15.

Notes

2. All the Wrong People

1. Another way of computing the Manhattan bias of price control benefits is to compare the aggregate windfall benefit of the Manhattan core resident to the rest of the city. In 1984 this was conservatively estimated to be worth $934 million for the Manhattan core's 308,000 controlled households ($3,032 per household) as opposed to $417 million per year for the city's remaining 848,000 controlled consumers ($492 per household per year) (Arthur D. Little, 1987).

2. Interview conducted in summer of 1985.

3. In 1985, the *American Housing Survey* conducted by the U.S. Commerce Department showed an average rental vacancy rate in U.S. cities of 5.7 percent and rates in certain selected cities as follows: Chicago, 7.5; St. Louis, 12.5; Baltimore, 8.8; Seattle, 8.3. Furthermore, the rental vacancy rate in New York has been declining in recent years. The official rate in New York in 1978 was 2.95 percent, and in 1965, 3.19 percent. See Stegman, 1988, for a history of New York City's vacancy rates.

4. There were 72,051 unavailable vacancies. We subtracted 6,241 dilapidated units, 899 being counted for non-residential use.

5. This includes 18,807 units undergoing renovation, and 3,414 rented but not yet occupied. ªThis includes 4,304 seasonally occupied units, 4,980 units held for occasional use, 4,906 units involved in legal disputes, and 17,692 units "held for other reasons."

6. Interview conducted in summer of 1985. The name has been changed.

4. A World of Adversaries

1. The RSA files are at the Rent Stabilization Association of New York City, Inc., 1600 Broadway, New York, NY 10036; research department, legal and press files. Access to files upon written request.

5. Once Upon a Time

1. The ten states without rent control during the war were Alaska, Idaho, Mississippi, Montana, Nevada, New Hampshire, North Dakota, South Dakota, Vermont, and Wyoming. This list is derived from Block, 1972.
2. In Connecticut, cities can exercise "jaw-boning" power to force landlords to limit rent increases, which most observers consider effective in restraining rents.
3. The states with state-wide prohibitions of local rent-control initiative are Arizona, Colorado, Florida, Georgia, Louisiana, Michigan, Minnesota, Mississippi, Missouri, North Carolina, Oklahoma, Oregon, South Carolina, Texas, Utah, and Washington (HUD, 1991).

6. Broken Promises

1. For a complete chronology of the rent control legislation in New York City, see Stegman, 1985.
2. The postwar rent-control laws did allow for an objective test, albeit an illusory one, by which rent control could have been lifted automatically. According to the 1951 rent-control law amendments, should any class of housing within the city obtain a vacancy rate of 5 percent or greater, that class would be decontrolled, since the original standard of the housing emergency would no longer be in effect. This provision, known as "statutory decontrol," was illusory because it was the controls themselves that created the housing shortage. Only by lifting the controls could the 5 percent vacancy threshold ever be reached. Even then, three categories of high-priced apartments were freed from controls by this provision in the "luxury decontrol" orders of 1957, 1960, and 1964. See Lett, 1976.
3. Keating, 1969, attributes the law's passage to four key factors: the political power of the middle and upper income tenants in the uncontrolled apartments, Mayor Lindsay's need for their votes in his 1969 re-election, the desire of tenant organizations to expand their political base, and the real estate industry's fear of a broadening of the rent-control system.

4. Between 1975 and 1987, the number of rent-controlled apartments declined from 642,000 to 155,000. As vacancies occur in rent-controlled apartments, rents are allowed to rise significantly, and subsequent increases in rent are then determined by rent stabilization. Moreover, the average age of tenants in the rent-controlled apartments has risen, and over half of the tenants in the controlled stock are now senior citizens. Barring some unforeseen changes in succession rights that might extend rent control to a new generation, the remaining rent-controlled apartments will eventually be vacated and put into rent stabilization.

8. The Hidden Tax

1. Several recent nationwide studies have shown that buildings in poorer neighborhoods are assessed at significantly higher rates relative to market value than those in better-off neighborhoods. Sternlieb and Lake found a severe property tax bias against poor neighborhoods in Pittsburgh (Sternlieb and Lake, 1976). Similarly, Peterson et al., 1973, found assessment rates in poor neighborhoods higher in eight of ten selected U.S. cities.

2. According to New York City Office of Management and Budget, 1987, tax abatements amounted to 13 percent of the total $4.89 billion in property tax receipts.

3. For a review of New York's constitutional limits on property tax, see Howe and Reeb, 1985. It should be noted that limitation is also flawed by the state's confusing definition of "full value." The value of property can be found by four methods: actual sale prices, comparison of sales prices of similar properties, net income capitalization, or replacement cost. While the city has recently begun using net income capitalization to value large apartment buildings, the prevalent valuation method is through comparing the sales price of comparable buildings. However, the state's sales comparison study takes three years to complete, leaving a large inflation component to take into account. The importance of the inflation component arises during the calculation of two different assessment rates: the *class ratios* (which we used earlier to calculate effective tax rates) and the *special equalization ratio*. The class ratio guides city tax assessors on what percentage of market value to assess and gives property owners a benchmark to challenge assessments. No inflation adjustment is used to compensate for the three-year lag in the sales study, allowing for a relatively high ratio of assessed to market value. The other assessment rate, the special equalization ratio, determines the "full value" of the tax base and hence the

2.5 percent tax limit (and coincidentally, the city's overall debt limit, too). Here, an 11.5 percent annual inflation factor is used, generating a relatively low ratio of assessed to market value, and hence allowing for a relatively high debt ceiling and tax limitation (New York State Board of Equalization and Assessment, p. 11).

To illustrate, suppose a property is assessed at $30,000. In calculating the *class ratio*, the State Board of Equalization relies upon a three-year old market value appraisal of $100,000 and finds a rate of 30 percent. In calculating its *special equalization ratio*, the Board adjusts the $100,000 appraisal to $139,000 and finds a ratio of 22 percent. Since these ratios conflict, one of two things must be happening. One possibility is that the class ratio is overstated and New York's effective tax rates (as reported earlier) are actually lower (25 percent lower if you believe the most recent special equalization ratio). The other possibility is that real estate inflation is less than 11.5 percent and the low special equalization ratio gives city officials an artificially high property tax ceiling.

In deciding which alternative to accept, we turn to yet another State Board of Equalization assessment rate, the *residential assessment rate*, which compares assessments to actual sales amounts for the same pieces of property. This rate is only calculated for Class I homeowner properties, since single family homes have by far the greatest degree of turnover and have enough observations to give consistent results. This rate is important because actual sales amounts *are* market values and allow us to generate actual assessment rates. This sales data shows at least for Class I, that the class ratios and equalization ratios are more accurate than the special equalization ratios and that the constitutional tax ceiling is much greater than the advertised 2.5 percent.

The purpose of this detailed description of New York assessment and equalization practices is to explain the ineffectiveness of current limitations on property tax rates and the conspicuous absence of any debate on the city's property tax policy. Moreover, the city's property tax rate(s) are adopted as a residual of past policy choices, not as a free variable. Each year, the mayor awaits certification from the state comptroller of the maximum possible property tax levy and what the appropriate share for each of the four classes should be. The tax share is then divided into each class's assessed valuation to get the four nominal tax rates. To illustrate how automatic this policy routine is: from 1975 to 1982, New York City *averaged* 96.2 percent of its constitutionally determined tax limit.

4. Under current law, property owners can challenge only the legality of their individual assessments, but cannot challenge the discriminatory

tax rates that the state law explicitly sanctions. And the vagueness of partial assessment tends to discourage most taxpayers from exercising their right to challenge assessments. For example, someone who owns an apartment building that he knows is worth $10 million will be unlikely to challenge an assessment of $7 million. He may think that he's getting a good deal, whereas in fact, $4 or $5 million may be more appropriate under current assessment practices.

9. Public Housing by Default

1. The maximum rent formula for public housing was later raised from 25 percent to 30 percent of the household's income.
2. Actually, the Section 8 program had two components, of which only the existing housing program represented a pure voucher. The Section 8 moderate rental rehabilitation program was actually a developers' subsidy program disguised as a voucher.
3. An exception to this rule is the city's 7A program, which allows a housing court to appoint a city administrator to manage a badly neglected apartment building should building code violations pose an immediate hazard to the tenants. Under this program, the administrator spends city money to make emergency repairs which the owner is obligated to reimburse (if he hopes to regain possession of the property).
4. Berenyi, 1989, credited New York City with spending $740 million on housing production and rehabilitation in fiscal year 1989. The remaining 50 cities in the study spent $198 million with the largest single amount, $50 million, spent by Los Angeles. On a per capita basis, New York City spent $102 per person compared to the next highest amount, $74, by Honolulu, and the 51-city average of $23 per person.

10. The State of the Debate

1. Of the 132,377 unregulated apartments not attributable to the city's inventory of small buildings or the co-op rentals, about 50,000 units are known to be part of the city's in rem stock, and as many as 5,000 are in single room occupancy facilities.
2. $121 = (1.10)^2 \times \$100$. $161 = (1.10)^5 \times \$100$.
3. Here we will make two important simplifications. First, we have removed the effect of future rent increases on the MCI increase. While this assumption will tend to make MCIs appear less profitable, the marginal analysis of changes in the interest rate still holds. Second, we have left out potential savings to the owner from reduced operating costs. Indeed, many of the MCIs are done for energy savings reasons.

This indicates that the current MCI formula may be insufficient, since successful improvements may need a source of revenue outside the formula. Now to calculate the present value of an MCI:

Let PV = the present value of the investment; R = the amount of rent increase; and i = the interest rate.

The formula for present value is:

(1) $PV = R + R/(1+i) + R/(1+i)^2 + R/(1+i)^3.$

(2) $PV \times (1+i) = R \times (1+i) + R + R/(1+i) + R/(1+i)^2 + R/(1+i)^3. \ldots$

Subtract (1) from (2):

(3) $PV \times (1+i) - PV = R \times (1+i).$

(4) $PV \times i = R \times (1+i).$

(4) $PV = R \times (1+i)/i.$

4. Suppose that the owner of a $500 per month apartment makes a major capital improvement whose cost equals or exceeds the MCI ceiling of $1,800 ($500 × 6 percent × 60 payments = $1,800). The rent increase that the owner would receive for his MCI would be $30 per month ($500 × 6 percent). Let us assume that the owner faces an interest rate of 12.7 percent, which translates into 1 percent per month. The first month's rent increase will occur as the investment is made and hence has a present value of $30. The second month's rent increase, however, will be worth 1 percent less to him, or $29.70, and the third month, 1.21 percent less, or $29.41. This sum of $30 rent increases continues indefinitely and reaches a present value of $3,030. In this case, R = $30 and i = .01. PV = $30 × 1.01/.01 = $3,030. Thus, the owner will make any investment approved by the DHCR that costs $3,030 or less, provided that the tenant does not move out and the interest rate does not rise. However, if interest rates were to grow to 2 percent per month or 26.8 percent per year, the present value of $30 per month is only $1,530. Since the $1,530 present value is less than the $1,800 cost, no owner would ever make a capital improvement under such conditions. For this reason, the MCI ceilings on monthly rent increases should be raised when high inflation and high interest rates prevail. Moreover, uncertainties surrounding MCI approval and changes in the MCI schedule may cause owners to ignore or discount the third, fourth, and subsequent years of MCI increases in their calculations, and not make investments that would otherwise appear profitable. Consider the tenant activists' proposal to roll back MCI rent increases after the 60-month period. Only $1,362 of the $3,030 present value of the rent increase occurs in the first five years. With so little return, capital investments would likely cease.

Appendix C

1. Homeless individuals do not show up in the Decennial Census or in the city's housing surveys. U.S. Census Bureau population counts are based on a listing or a sample of homes and a count of households or housed individuals. While the Bureau attempted a nation-wide street population count as part of the 1990 Census, there were no previous numbers to compare their new count with. The only count of street populations over time, from Nashville, Tennessee, shows no dramatic increase in homeless population between 1983 and 1988 (though of course the situation in New York may be very different).

   Because of this information vacuum, describing New York's homeless population requires extrapolating from municipal studies of the existing shelter population. For example, in 1983, the New York State Department of Social Services conducted a survey of all known shelter providers in New York State, asking them the maximum, minimum, and average number of homeless people sheltered on a given night. The survey found an average of 16,699 homeless people were sheltered in New York City in 1983.

   To estimate the total number of homeless in the city, we must rely upon one of a number of published estimates of the ratio of street homeless to sheltered homeless. In its 1984 report, the U.S. Department of Housing and Urban Development found 1.3 street homeless for every shelter homeless in studies from Boston and Pittsburgh, and 2.7 to 1 from a Phoenix study (the different ratio often attributed to Phoenix's warmer climate). A study done for the National Bureau of Economic Research found a ratio of 2.32 to 1 among the homeless in New York City (although the study relied upon a non-random survey of street homeless). On the basis of these three studies, the total number of homeless in New York City could be estimated at 38,400, or 53,900, or 61,800. Confounding these estimates is the increasing number of persons being sheltered the New York City system. Between 1984 and 1987, the number of individuals and family members in city-run shelters almost doubled. Since 1987, approximately 27,000 persons on an average night have stayed at a city shelter. However, to assume from these numbers that the overall number of homeless have been rising raises two questions. First, is this increase in sheltered population due to changing economic and social conditions or to a change in policy? Second, if the sheltered population is rising so rapidly, has the street-to-shelter ratio remained constant? (Lee, 1989; New York State Department of Social Services, 1984; U.S. Department of Housing and Urban Development, 1984; Freeman and Hall, 1986; New York City, Office of the Mayor, 1989)

Index